MANAGING YOURSELF

PRACTICAL HELP FOR CHRISTIANS IN PERSONAL
PLANNING, TIME SCHEDULING AND SELF-CONTROL

MANAGING YOURSELF

PRACTICAL HELP FOR CHRISTIANS IN PERSONAL
PLANNING, TIME SCHEDULING AND SELF-CONTROL

STEPHEN B. DOUGLASS
FOREWORD BY BILL BRIGHT

CAMPUS CRUSADE FOR CHRIST INTERNATIONAL

———————

MANAGING YOURSELF is a Campus Crusade for Christ book, published by:

Here's Life Publishers, Inc.
A Ministry of Campus Crusade for Christ
P. O. Box 1576
San Bernardino, CA 92402

Second printing, September 1982
Third printing, August 1984
Fourth printing, April 1985

ISBN 0-918956-49-8   40-09-03
Library of Congress 78-70647

FOR MORE INFORMATION, WRITE:

L.I.F.E. — P.O. Box A399, Sydney South 2000, Australia
Campus Crusade for Christ of Canada — Box 300, Vancouver, B.C., V6C 2X3, Canada
Campus Crusade for Christ — 103 Friar Street, Reading RGI IEP, Berkshire, England
Lay Institute for Evangelism — P.O. Box 8786, Auckland 3, New Zealand
Great Commission Movement of Nigeria — P.O. Box 500, Jos, Plateau State Nigeria, West Africa
Life Ministry — P.O. Box/Bus 91015, Auckland Park 2006, Republic of South Africa
Campus Crusade for Christ International — Arrowhead Springs, San Bernardino, CA 92414, U.S.A.

To my mother and father

Contents

Part II
Beyond the Basics: Tools for Further Effectiveness

Acknowledgments

On Good Friday, March 24, 1978, my father went home to be with the Lord. The day before he had finished helping me with a section of this book. I would be grossly remiss if I did not gratefully acknowledge first, not only his specific help with the book, but also the powerful role both he and my mother have had in getting me started learning about personal management. I witnessed their using "to do" lists, working hard to complete projects, and not settling for a job poorly done. They exhorted and encouraged me as I grew up.

To my wife, Judy, I express my thanks for her encouragement to me to write, her patience with me while I did write, and her example to me in how well she manages herself. I further express my thanks to her for doing the final edit on the finished manuscript.

To Cathy Hustedt I am deeply grateful for her tireless, thorough work in editing the entire book. Her sharp mind and intense desire for the concepts to be expressed clearly contributed greatly to what you will read.

To Rolland Dingman goes my appreciation for his illustrations that make the message much clearer and more easily remembered.

To Fred West I express my thanks for his research, comments and general availability to help.

To Vicki See, Sally Edgar, Bev Austin, Cris Holler, and Diana Heddens I give special thanks for the many volunteer hours spent typing.

To the John Lynches and the Bo Bottomlys I express my appreciation for quiet get-aways at crucial points in the writing and the editing.

Foreword

Steve Douglass, both by his godly, well-ordered life and efficient, effective ministry, is eminently qualified to author this excellent, provocative book, *Managing Yourself*.

All of us, at one point or another in our lives, have felt the need for more time. We cannot seem to squeeze all we would like to do into 24 hours a day. Sometimes we find ourselves pressured or anxious because our lives are crowded with many activities, yet there are important things we just never get around to doing.

If any of these have ever been your experiences, I feel this book is for you. Steve Douglass has put together a book that will be useful no matter what your occupation because it contains practical suggestions and because it is based on solid biblical principles. It has been my privilege to work closely with Steve for nine years. During this time, he has made a vital contribution to the Lord's work through Campus Crusade for Christ, serving for several years as Vice President for Administration. I have observed that he consistently applies the principles described in his book in both his professional and personal life.

In a deeper dimension I would also recommend this book because as Christians we should seek to maximize our time for the Lord. His Word tells us, "So be careful how you act; these are difficult days. Don't be fools; be wise: make the most of every opportunity you have for doing good" (Ephesians 5:15,16, Living Bible). *Managing Yourself* will help you be sure that you are living each day of your life in such a way that you will bring the most glory to God.

Bill Bright
President and Founder
Campus Crusade for Christ International

PART I
The Basics of
Managing Yourself

Introduction

Have you ever heard the story about the farmer who told his wife one morning that he was going out to plow the "south forty"? He got off to an early start so he could oil the tractor. He needed more oil, so he went to the shop to get it. On the way to the shop, he noticed the pigs weren't fed. So he proceeded to the corncrib, where he found some sacks of feed. The sacks reminded him that his potatoes were sprouting. When he started for the potato pit, he passed the woodpile and remembered that his wife wanted wood in the house. As he picked up a few sticks, an ailing chicken passed by. He dropped the wood and reached for the chicken. When evening arrived, the frustrated farmer had not even gotten to the tractor, let alone to the field!

How many times have you found yourself in a similar situation? You intended to do something you knew was important, but were distracted and never accomplished what you set out to do.

Or perhaps you can think of something that you have always wanted to do but can never find time for. By the same token, are you aware of something that you do often that is a waste of time? If you are a normal person, you answered "yes" to both questions and thought of something specific in each case. Isn't it strange that we can want to do one thing for a long time and never get to it, and yet at the same time freely admit we are wasting time on other activities? That is why we need to learn to manage ourselves.

Demands on Our Time

We are all faced with many, many demands on our time. The boss wants that project now, the telephone rings throughout the day, people drop in unexpectedly at home or at the office, the television tells us that we should be enjoying all sorts of pleasant activities, the pastor encourages us to become more involved, the kids want to play baseball, the family wants to go out to eat . . . Sound familiar?

There are so many choices. And yet we alone must decide what to do next. We may decide in response to circumstances. We may decide in response to obligations we feel to people. We may decide out of habit or tradition. We may do only what we enjoy. Or, we may make purposeful, God-inspired decisions. One way or the other, we decide.

In this world of high pace and complexity it would certainly help us if we learned to be good managers or stewards of ourselves. The principles set forth in this book are intended to help you to make more effective use of your time and your other resources.

Most People Drift Through Life

I am sadly convinced that most people basically drift through life. They go to school because the law requires it and their friends are there. They get a job in order to put food on the table and gas in the car. They get married because everyone else has and they're getting lonesome. They buy a home, join a church, watch TV, raise the kids and retire—all because these activities seem the "normal" thing to do.

Instead of seeking God's specific direction for these and other courses of action, many people tend to proceed through life without much prayer or thought and, therefore, without God's integrating purpose.

I have seen many people reflect back on the activities of their past and conclude that most were basically meaningless and worthless in terms of accomplishing God's purpose for their lives. Perhaps they chose the wrong career, or married the wrong person, or settled in the wrong community—all because they didn't listen to God and really pursue His direction.

God Expects Good Management of Self

Do you remember the parable of the talents as it is recounted in Matthew 25:14-30? Jesus tells a story of a master who gave three of his servants money (talents) to invest while he was away. To one he gave five talents; to another, two; and to the third servant, one talent. When the master returned, he asked all three to account for the money. The servants who had received five and two talents, respectively, were rewarded, for both had doubled their talents through wise investments. The third servant, however, had done nothing with his talent. Because of this poor performance, no reward was given and, in fact, his talent was taken away from him and he was punished.

One of the main lessons to be learned here for us as Christians is that God **expects** us to fruitfully invest whatever He gives us. Often we think of God's blessings in terms of money or material goods. But time is also a gift of God, one that He has given all of us equally each day, and we are expected, in fact, **commanded**, to use it wisely. "Therefore be careful how you walk, not as unwise men, but as wise, making the most of your time, because the days are evil" (Ephesians 5:15,16).

Good Time Management Is Possible

Fortunately for all of us, God is well aware of our tendency to drift amidst the jet-stream of circumstances and possibilities in life, and so, along with commanding us to invest our time wisely, He has made it possible for us to do so. The ninth part of the fruit of the Spirit is **self-control** (Galatians 5:23), and in the original Greek of the New Testament, this term means "controlling power." By trusting God and walking in His Spirit (which we will learn more about in Chapter 2), we can actually be empowered to exert control over how our time is invested.

It is truly exciting that God **intends** for us to live this way. As with other parts of the fruit of the Spirit, however, we need to trust God to make this area of self-control an increasingly active and effective part of our lives.

God offers each one of us a wonderful plan for our lives. In John 10:10 Jesus says, "I came that they might have life and have it abundantly." Managing yourself involves discovering that plan and implementing it. As you think about it, do you really want anything less out of life?

Methods of Managing Yourself

My chief objective in writing this book is to help you better manage the life God has given you. It is my desire that, at the minimum, you learn the following:

1. How to set objectives for your life.

2. How to determine the area of your life in which you most want to see accomplishment or improvement in the next six to twelve months, and then how to determine the best way to achieve that accomplishment or improvement.

3. How to schedule each day in order to accomplish your highest priorities.

4. How to follow through on what you actually plan for each day.

5. How to walk more closely with God and listen to His directions.

My desire is that you not only learn **about** these processes, but that you actually **work on** at least some of them during the course of your reading. For it is far better to **apply** one or two of the procedures than just to learn about all of them.

A Simple but Powerful Formula

I have discovered a threefold formula for handling the problems, decisions, opportunities, new information, etc., that come into my life. This simple but powerful formula involves prayer, thought and action, in that order.

First, I trust God for His special provision of wisdom and power in the circumstance.

Next, I assume that God is already beginning to work in my mind as I try to think out solutions, decisions, responses, etc. There are many techniques that help in this process, and these will be detailed in the chapters ahead.

Last, I seek to implement, for a solution thought through is still not a solution accomplished. As James advises, " ... prove yourselves **doers** of the word, and not merely hearers ... " (James 1:22).

Let me say again that the purpose of this book is to actually help you manage yourself better. The changing of life attitudes and habits takes time for all of us. You can read great amounts of material on this subject and still not see changes in your life if you never make the effort to apply what you've read to your own circumstances. Since you probably will never be more equipped nor more motivated to implement a concept than just after you've read it, I would urge you to put this book down from time to time, as appropriate, in order to pray, think through and apply.

When you come to a concept which you feel would especially fill a need in your life, stop your reading and really focus on that one concept. Ask God for creative ideas to make it a part of your life. You might, for example, place reminders to yourself about it at home and at work. At any rate, try to do something every day, however small, toward making that one concept a part of your life. Pray for the personal motivation and discipline to keep at it until the process becomes a habit. Remember, too, to thank God for working in your life in this way.

A Book in Two Parts

As a help to comprehension, this book is divided into two basic parts. Part I is designed to teach you simply and quickly the basic concepts of managing yourself. If you were able to read only this part of the book, you should come away with information that, if applied, should substantially improve your effectiveness and satisfaction in life.

Part II presents information that supplements what you've learned in Part I and is designed to give the interested reader a more in-depth learning experience on the various topics introduced in Part I. For example, in the chapter concerning planning in Part I, you are encouraged to start thinking about your life objectives by simply jotting down on paper the thoughts that first occur to you.

In Part II, this process is carried much further and you are given a great deal of material relative to planning for various specific areas in your life. You should be stimulated here to think of personal needs that may not have occurred to you in Part I.

Chapter 2 presents the spiritual prerequisites to managing yourself. I cannot overemphasize the importance of these prerequisites, all of which concern the vitality of your relationship with God. Your walk with God is by far the most significant factor in how well you manage yourself.

2

The Spiritual Prerequisites to Managing Yourself

I am often asked how to know God's will concerning some opportunity or problem. My answer always starts with the statement: "If you walk closely with God, you will know and do His will." Of all the ways to make the most of your life that we will be discussing in this book, none is more effective than the maintaining of a close, moment-by-moment walk with God.

God Is Available for Advice

To see why this is so, let us consider the nature of God. Among other things, He is the Creator-God of the universe, eternal, all wise, all powerful. He is the truth, so that every word He utters is entirely reliable. He is all loving and all kind, so that He is concerned with the well-being of His children.

Now doesn't it stand to reason that a God such as this, knowing everything there is to know about everything, knows very well how you should be spending your time?

And doesn't it follow that, since He wants the best for

your life, God is willing, even eager, to share that knowledge with you? Indeed it does!

The Bible confirms that God intends to help us make the most of our lives. Consider, for example, the promise of Psalms 32:8 as recorded in the Living Bible: "I will instruct you (says the Lord) and guide you along the best pathway for your life; I will advise you and watch your progress." The Bible further assures us that God is available for consultation on any matter, great or small, on a regular basis: "But if any of you lacks wisdom, let Him ask of God, who gives to all men generously and without reproach, and it will be given to him" (James 1:5).

"Ask, and it shall be given to you; seek, and you shall find; knock, and it shall be opened to you" (Matthew 7:7).

God knows what is best for us and He cares for us. All we really need to do is ask in faith for His wisdom for our lives.

We Ignore Him

Unbelievable as it seems, many Christians totally ignore the day-to-day wisdom God offers.

Even relatively "devout" Christians pray only a few times during the day—at morning devotions, before meals and at bedtime—and their prayers at these times are usually in the form of giving thanks rather than requests for wisdom.

Many other Christians consult God only in time of trouble. When they have done their best and that is not enough, then they think to call on God, requesting a miracle, or special discernment in a difficult situation. How many times have you heard the statement, "Although I have never been much of a praying person, in that circumstance I asked God to . . . and told Him that in return I would . . . for the rest of my life"?

Many Christians sacrifice great amounts of time and money, travel long distances and go through mental agony for years in order to attain some higher level of education, and yet do not bother to ask God for a portion of His infinite wisdom.

Isn't it incredible? Here we have the privilege of relating to and fellowshiping with God and of benefiting from His wisdom on any matter at any time (Hebrews 10:19) and more often than not we fail to take advantage of it.

How to Walk with God

For many, perhaps, it is a matter of not knowing how to relate to God. In the remainder of this chapter, I would like to share with you four concepts that can strengthen your walk with God:
1. Being sure you are a Christian
2. Experiencing God's love and forgiveness
3. Being filled with the Spirit
4. Walking in the Spirit

This material is adapted from a series of booklets called the Transferable Concepts, by Dr. Bill Bright, published by Campus Crusade for Christ, Inc. These concepts truly are prerequisites to managing yourself in accordance with God's plan.

PREREQUISITE NO. 1: Being Sure You Are a Christian

The first of the spiritual prerequisites to managing yourself successfully is to be sure of your relationship with Christ. For if you are not a Christian, you will simply not have access to the wisdom and guidance which God provides for those who believe in Him. And if you are not **sure** of your position in Christ, you will hesitate to entrust yourself to Him as you should to gain that wisdom and guidance.

What is involved in becoming a Christian? It involves agreeing with God concerning the fact that you have sinned (Romans 3:23) and that this sin separates you from God (Romans 6:23). It involves recognizing that Christ died in your place (Romans 5:8) and inviting Him to come into your life (Revelation 3:20) and forgive your sins (Ephesians 1:7; I Corinthians 15:3), thereby bridging the chasm between you and God (John 14:6). If you can say that you have come to the point that you have asked Christ into your life and are trusting in God's forgiveness through Christ, then you can **know** you are a Christian.

Trustworthiness of God and His Word

Foremost among the assurances that you are a Christian is the trustworthiness of God and His Word. Jesus said in Revelation 3:20, "Behold, I stand at the door and knock; if any one hears My voice and opens the door, I will come in to him . . . . " Because of the perfect character of God, we can know without doubt that, when He says He will do something, He will, in fact, do it. Therefore, if through an act of your will you sincerely opened the door of your heart to Christ, you can know that He has actually entered your life, for He would not deceive you.

The Presence of God in Our Lives

Now the trustworthiness of God and His Word is an external witness to the fact that you are a Christian. You also can sense God's presence in your life. We are told in I John 5:10, "The one who believes in the Son of God has the witness **in himself** . . . " (emphasis mine).

One of the functions of God's Spirit in your life is to teach you the things of God, to illuminate them for you and to bring them to memory as needed. Have you ever been reading the Bible and had a certain thought you hadn't noticed before seem to literally jump up from the page and come to life? That is probably the work of the Holy Spirit in your life. Does it seem unusual to you that the Bible, a book which you once considered boring and irrelevant, has become extremely interesting and meaningful to you since becoming a Christian? Again, this is the doing of the Holy Spirit. Have you ever been constrained from doing something because, just as you were about to do it, a verse of Scripture suddenly came to mind and you realized the activity was wrong? Again, this is the work of the Holy Spirit in you.

If these kinds of things are happening in your life, they testify to the fact that you are, indeed, a Christian.

If Christ has entered your life, you can also expect to see positive changes in your life—to the extent that you trust Him for these changes. It is God's purpose to conform you to the image of His Son (Romans 8:29) and that involves changes for all of us.

After I became a Christian, and particularly after I learned to trust God moment by moment, my own life began to change, sometimes in ways that I hadn't even anticipated. My thoughts began to change; many of my actions changed. And I had an increasing desire to obey and to please God. You should be experiencing some of these kinds of things in your own life. You can, of course, refuse to trust God to implement changes in your life. If you do refuse, as a Christian, you will find yourself very frustrated and unhappy. And this, too, is a testimony of God's presence in your life.

You Can Become a Christian

Now it may be that, as you have been reading about how to become a Christian and how to be assured of your relationship with God, you have realized that you are not a Christian. You can receive Jesus Christ into your life right now by simply acknowledging the fact that there is sin in your life which needs to be forgiven and by asking Him to enter your life and to make you what He wants you to be. "But **as many as received Him**, to them He gave the right to become children of God, even to those who believe in His name" (John 1:12, emphasis mine).

The following is a suggested prayer: "Lord Jesus, I need You. I open the door of my life and receive You as my Savior and Lord. Thank You for forgiving my sins. Take control of my life. Make me the kind of person You want me to be."

If this prayer expresses your desire, pray it now and ask Christ to come into your life and establish your relationship with God.

If you just prayed that prayer, reread this section on Being

Sure You Are a Christian before going on. Write Campus
Crusade for Christ, San Bernardino, CA 92414 for further
help and information.

PREREQUISITE NO. 2: Experiencing God's Love and Forgiveness

Relationship vs. Fellowship

When you became a Christian, you entered into a father-
child type of relationship with God (John 1:12). You also
entered into a potential for close fellowship with God. As a
Christian, you can talk with God directly and receive His
directions concerning the pathway that is best for you
(Psalms 32:8).

When you sin, your **relationship** with God is not broken.
You don't cease being God's spiritual child any more than
you cease being your human parents' child when you do
something they don't like.

However, your close **fellowship** with God is disrupted
when you sin. In I John 1 the word used to describe fellowship with God in the original language means "to share in
common." When we sin, we cease living in a way that is
totally "shared in common" with God (I John 1:5,6). We are
not anxious to talk to God because we feel guilty and embarrassed by our sin. Our fellowship with Him has grown cold.

Confession Is the Solution

Fortunately, God anticipated that we probably would sin
(I John 2:1) and has provided a way for us to experience
His forgiveness and to be restored to close fellowship with
Him. I John 1:9 states, "If we confess our sins, He is faithful
and righteous to forgive us our sins and to cleanse us from
all unrighteousness." The word for "confess" in the original
language means to "speak the same thing" or to "agree
with." If sin illustrates that we are out of agreement (not in
common) with God on a matter, then we must come back

into agreement with God to restore fellowship.

Whereas your guilty feelings over sin tend to make you not want to talk to God, you must talk to Him to experience His love and forgiveness. When you confront God "face to face" with what you have done, agreeing with Him that it is wrong, and repenting of your wrong action or attitude, then you open the floodgates of God's love and forgiveness which pour into your heart. This is a forgiveness you usually can feel—as a sense of relief and well-being—as well as something you can know intellectually on the basis of God's promise. This confession of a sin includes a genuine regret for having committed it and a sincere desire to refrain from doing it again. Simply acknowledging that something is a sin with the full intention of repeating it doesn't bring the flood of forgiveness.

Take Care of Your Sins

Perhaps you have been a Christian for some time, and God does not seem to be working in your life. It could well be that some unconfessed sins have put up a barrier between you and God and have cut short His efforts on your behalf.

If that is the case, why not take care of this right now? First, ask God to reveal to you sins you have not confessed to Him. Write all of them on a sheet of paper. Don't be introspective; just jot down the sins that God brings to your mind. When you have completed your list, write out across it God's promise in I John 1:9: "If we confess our sins, He is faithful and righteous to forgive us our sins and to cleanse us from all unrighteousness."

Now, if you agree with God that the things you have listed are sin, and if you are truly sorry for your wrong actions or thoughts, and if you honestly say to God that, though you are weak and might do the things again, it is your genuine desire not to do them, then you can thank Him for forgiving your sins on the basis of Christ's death for them.

Ask God to guide you in seeking forgiveness from others concerning any of these sins. Then, destroy your list, knowing that you are forgiven.

PREREQUISITE NO. 3: Being Filled with the Spirit

Can you relate to the plight of the apostle Paul? Here is his problem: "No matter which way I turn I can't make myself do right. I want to but I can't. When I want to do good, I don't; and when I try not to do wrong, I do it anyway . . . It seems to be a fact of life that when I want to do what is right, I inevitably do what is wrong" (excerpted from Romans 7:18-21, Living Bible).

Not in Our Own Strength

In Romans 8, Paul states that man was never intended to live the Christian life in his own strength. Even the best-intentioned and most highly disciplined among us will eventually give in to temptation and fall short of the mark. Our old sin nature will thwart our good intentions.

If that is the case, then why does God hold up to us standards that are impossible to meet? The answer lies in the fact that God doesn't want us to live the Christian life at all; He wants to live the Christian life in us and through us.

To understand this concept, let's back up a moment to whenever it was that you became a Christian. When you received Christ into your life, you actually received God's Spirit also (Ephesians 1:13,14; Colossians 2:9,10). The Holy Spirit has all of the resources that are needed to live the Christian life: the power, the wisdom, the constant availability.

Now that is the power source which God wants us to draw on as we seek to live the Christian life. In fact, in Ephesians 5:18, God actually commands us to be "filled with the Holy Spirit," that is to say, we are commanded to be directed and empowered by the Holy Spirit.

Two Types of Christian

In I Corinthians 2:15-3:3 we learn that a Christian can be in one of two states: spiritual or carnal (man of flesh). In Campus Crusade for Christ, we like to illustrate these two possibilities with the following circles:

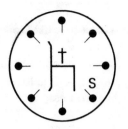

SPIRITUAL CHRISTIAN   CARNAL CHRISTIAN

† = Christ

S = Self

● = Activity in the life

⊓ = Throne or control center of the life

The circles represent the lives of the two types of Christian. Each person has received Christ, as indicated by the respective crosses inside the circles. The spiritual Christian has put Christ on the throne of his life; that is to say, he is allowing Christ to run his life as he is directed and empowered by the Holy Spirit.

The carnal Christian has placed himself on the throne of his life; he is running his life by himself without the benefit of God's direction and power. Notice that in the life of the spiritual Christian, the activities, as represented by the dots, are in balance. This represents the peace, joy, and purpose enjoyed by a person in harmony with God's plan. The interests of the carnal Christian are in disarray, representing the discord and frustration resulting from not being in harmony with God's plan.

Now which of these circles represents your life? Is it the circle on the left? Some of the characteristics of the spiritual Christian include: He is Christ-centered and empowered by the Holy Spirit, introduces others to Christ, has an effective prayer life, understands God's Word, is able to trust God and to obey Him, and he increasingly exhibits the fruit of the Spirit in his life as he matures and trusts Christ to develop them. The fruit, as recorded in Galatians 5:22,23, is love, joy, peace, patience, kindness, goodness, faithfulness, gentleness and self-control.

Or is your life best represented by the circle on the right? The carnal Christian is often characterized by unbelief, disobedience, a poor prayer life, an up-and-down spiritual experience, no desire for Bible study, impure thoughts, jealousy, guilt, worry, discouragement, frustration, aimlessness.

Become a Spiritual Christian

If you can relate to the circle on the right, and yet you sincerely desire a Christ-controlled life, there is no reason you cannot take care of that right now. The prerequisites include a sincere desire to be controlled and empowered by the Holy Spirit, the confession of your sins and the faith to simply claim the filling of the Holy Spirit according to God's command to be filled in Ephesians 5:18 and His promise in I John 5:14,15 that He will grant your requests when you pray according to His will.

Why not take time right now to confess your sins, if you have not already done so, and to ask God to take control of the throne of your life? Ask Him to fill you with the Holy Spirit in accordance with His command, and **know** that He will do so because your request is made in accordance with His will. Your authority is the trustworthiness of God and His Word.

Finally, thank God for filling you with His Spirit as He promised to do, and then get on with the business of living, trusting God to lead you along the pathway He knows is best for you, trusting Him to conform you increasingly to the image of His Son and trusting Him to provide the power to live as He wants you to live.

PREREQUISITE NO. 4: Walking in the Spirit

Is Sin Still Possible?

Now the question is, if Christ is on the throne of your life and you are being controlled and empowered by the Holy Spirit, is it possible for you to sin, thereby disrupting your fellowship with God? The answer is "yes," because, even though you have yielded the control of your life to Christ, your ego is still very much alive. That is to say, you still have freedom of choice; you can disregard Christ's control and do what **you** want at any time.

When you **do** disregard Christ's direction, your sin is really twofold; for you are first removing Christ from His position of leadership in your life and you then are committing whatever else it is that is contrary to His Will.

Be Continually Filled

Unlike the indwelling of the Spirit then, which occurs when you become a Christian, the filling of the Spirit is not a one-time, irrevocable occurrence. In God's command in Ephesians 5:18, the verb used in the original Greek for the filling of the Spirit means to be **constantly** or **continually** filled. Therefore, when you remove Christ from the throne of your life through sin, it is both possible and necessary to restore Him to His rightful position by being filled with the Spirit again.

This new filling takes place in the same way as before. You confess your sin to God, agreeing with Him that it is wrong, and experience His forgiveness on the basis of Christ's sacrifice 2,000 years ago, remembering that confession involves repentance—a genuine remorse for having committed the wrongdoing and a desire to avoid a repeat performance. You then resurrender the control of your life to Christ and appropriate the filling of the Holy Spirit by faith, in accordance with God's command to be filled and His promise to grant any requests made in accordance with His will.

Spiritual Breathing

This process could be described as "spiritual breathing." When you breathe physically, you exhale the impure air and you inhale the pure. When you breathe spiritually, you "exhale" through the confession of your sin, and you "inhale" by appropriating the fullness of the Holy Spirit by faith.

This is an ongoing process, one to be repeated whenever sin occurs in your life. The more mature Christian may need to breathe spiritually only occasionally, whereas the newer Christian may find that He must repeat the process often. However, if that new Christian sees to it that he is continually Spirit filled, God will be free to work in his life for good, bringing him to maturity.

In fact, as you walk with God, breathing spiritually as needed, you can expect the following types of things to be true of your life: You will demonstrate more and more of the fruit of the Spirit (Galatians 5:22,23) and be increasingly conformed to the image of Christ (Romans 12:2; II Corinthians 3:18). Your prayer life and the study of God's Word will become more meaningful; you will experience God's power in witnessing (Acts 1:8); you will be prepared for spiritual conflict against the world (I John 2:15-17), against the flesh (Galatians 5:16,17) and against Satan (I Peter 5:7-9; Ephesians 6:10-13); and you will increasingly experience God's power to resist temptation and sin (I Corinthians 10:13; Philippians 4:13; Ephesians 1:19-23; 6:10; II Timothy 1:7; Romans 6:1-16). In short, you will be equipped to manage yourself in a way you never dreamed possible and you will be able to know and implement God's plan for your life.

3

Planning Long Range

"Do you not know that those who run in a race all run, but only one receives the prize? Run in such a way that you may win. And everyone who competes in the games exercises self-control in all things. They then do it to receive a perishable wreath, but we an imperishable. Therefore I run in such a way, as not without aim; I box in such a way as not beating the air" (I Corinthians 9:24-26). Paul tells us that to win in life we must proceed with purpose.

How many sprinters have you seen line up in their starting blocks, get ready to run, take off with the gun and proceed two or three steps, then suddenly stop and look around for the finish line? Of course, you have never seen that, have you? Why? Because any sprinter in his right mind would figure out where the finish line was long before starting the race. Otherwise, he wouldn't stand a chance of winning.

And yet, how many of us, in the race of life, get 30, 40, 50 years down the road without any concept of where the finish line is for us? I am not speaking here of heaven, but rather of the sum total that God wants to see accomplished by the end of our lives. To get to this finish line successfully, we must be pointed and progressing in the right direction. Put another way, we must **plan**.

I'm sure that the term "planning" is familiar to you. We all use the word frequently. We plan to go downtown. We have certain plans for this evening. We make plans for our vacations and for many other things. Usually, however, we do not give much thought to our long-range future, and therefore we often end up disappointed with the results of our lives.

The Bible has a lot to say on why we, as Christians, should plan. I would like to direct your attention now to three of these reasons:

Planning Leads to Order

In the first place, Christians should plan because planning leads to the kind of orderly lives that God intends for us to lead. In I Corinthians 14:40 we are commanded to " . . . let all things be done properly and in an orderly manner."

Have you ever gone all the way downtown to the store and returned only to discover that you forgot to stop at the cleaners on the way? This sort of thing can happen in your work if you proceed in a haphazard manner. You can forget to book a speaker for a conference until it is too late, or you can get started on a project only to find out that you don't have the right tools. Planning can help eliminate this kind of disorder.

Christ Advocated Thinking Ahead

In the second place, Christians should plan because Christ advocated thinking ahead. To help explain the careful forethought a person should give toward becoming a disciple, Jesus used the following illustration:

> "For which one of you, when he wants to build
> a tower, does not first sit down and calculate the
> cost, to see if he has enough to complete it?
> Otherwise, when he has laid a foundation, and
> is not able to finish, all who observe it begin to

ridicule him, saying, 'This man began to build and was not able to finish.' Or what king, when he sets out to meet another king in battle, will not first sit down and take counsel whether he is strong enough with ten thousand men to encounter the one coming against him with twenty thousand? Or else, while the other is still far away, he sends a delegation and asks terms of peace" (Luke 14:28-32).

God Desires to Give Direction

In the third place, Christians should plan because God desires to give direction to our lives. In Psalms 32:8, the Lord tells us, "I will instruct you and teach you in the way which you should go; I will counsel you with my eye upon you." Psalms 37:23 confirms that "the steps of a man are established by the Lord . . . . "

If we allow Him, God will provide us with guidelines for living that are custom-tailored to our individual lives. For He has established a plan for each of us that fits in with His overall plan.

Overview

In this chapter you will learn the beginnings of how to plan for your personal life. By the time you finish the chapter you should have:

1. Written down objectives for your life.
2. Selected one specific area of accomplishment or im-improvement in your life that you most want to emphasize in the next six to twelve months.
3. Determined the best way to achieve that accomplishment or improvement.

What you learn and apply in this chapter sets the direction that the next three chapters help you implement. If you are headed in no particular direction or in the wrong direction, no amount of efficiency helps you achieve your objective. If you know you are headed in the right direction, every step takes you closer to your objective.

The purpose of this chapter is to cause you to apply as much personal planning as possible in a short period of time. See Chapter 8 in Part II for more complete explanation and application concerning the planning process, the establishment of life objectives and six-to-twelve-month objectives, and the implementation of these objectives.

How to Plan

Planning involves five steps:
1. Pray (Appropriate God's wisdom for your plan.)
2. Establish objectives (Determine **what** should be accomplished.)
3. Program (Determine **how** the objectives should be accomplished.)
4. Schedule (Determine **when** each activity in the plan should be accomplished.)
5. Budget (Determine **how much** manpower, money and other resources will be needed and **how** they should be supplied.)

This process can be applied to a large organization, a project, a meeting or an individual life. Instead of explaining further about the process at this point, however, I would like for you to have a chance to try out a few of the steps in planning for your personal life.

First Pray

No doubt you want the best possible plan for your life. Only God knows what that is. Yet He will enlighten our minds with His wisdom, if we will only ask: "But if any of you lacks wisdom, let him ask God, who gives to all men generously and without reproach, and it will be given to him" (James 1:5).

Pause now and ask God for His wisdom. Ask Him for His overall direction in your life. Ask Him for His area of special emphasis in your life in the next six to twelve months. Ask Him for the best way to accomplish that emphasis.

Determine Your Life Objectives

Expect God to be enlightening your mind as you proceed. Thank Him as He does.

As I have searched the Scriptures, I have come to the conclusion that the basic objective in life for Christians is to glorify God. The psalmists exemplified it in their psalms (e.g., Psalms 96); Jesus accomplished it in His earthly life (John 17:4), and it is the main emphasis in heaven (Isaiah 6:3; Revelation 4:8-11).

John 15:8 suggests how to glorify God, "By this is My Father glorified, that you bear much fruit, and so prove to be My disciples." The main way we can glorify God is to be a disciple of Jesus, increasingly conforming to His image (Romans 8:29) and obeying Him. Bearing "fruit" suggests two specific ways to glorify God: Disciple Christians and share the gospel with non-Christians. As we minister to Christians, we see the fruit of the Spirit (Galatians 5:22,23) increasingly manifested in their lives. As we introduce others to Christ, we see fruit in the sense of harvest. These thoughts may be of help to you as you determine your life objectives.

Take out paper and pencil and write down what you hope to accomplish in your lifetime. This should include not only what God has called all Christians to accomplish, but it also should include what He has specifically called you to do. What specific strengths and opportunities has He given to you in life? How can they best contribute to His overall objective for you as a Christian? (See Chapter 9—"Knowing God's Will for Your life"—if you want further help in answering these last two questions.) Pause now and write down your thoughts concerning your life objectives.

Determine a Shorter-term Objective

Your life objectives give overall direction to your activities. You will probably also be helped, though, by determining one objective to specifically emphasize over the next six to twelve months. This could be a specific accomplishment such as completing a large project. It could be a specific improvement you would like to see in your life such as Bible study and prayer becoming a regular, meaningful activity for you each morning. This objective should be the accomplishment or improvement that is the highest priority to you. In other words, what is the one thing you would really like to see happen in the next six to twelve months? It may have occurred to you while you were thinking about your life objective. It may be something you have been meaning to do, but haven't found the time. Pause now and write down your highest priority objective for the next six to twelve months.

Determine the Best Program

Next, you need to determine how best to accomplish your six-to-twelve-month objective. If you are a natural planner, you can proceed to step out the sequence of activities that will take you from where you are now to the point where the objective is accomplished. If you are not such a natural at planning, you will probably find the following procedure helpful.

List several things you could do that would contribute in some way toward accomplishing your six-to-twelve-month objective. If improving your Bible study and prayer habits is your objective, you might read a book on the subject, listen to a tape or record, enroll in a course (correspondence or live), buy a more current translation of the Bible (if you have trouble understanding the one you have), go to bed earlier in the evening (if you can't seem to squeeze in the time in the morning), consult with a friend who does well in this area. Depending on your circumstances, all of these and others might be ways for you to improve in this area. Pause now and create such a list for your objective.

Now select from this list the one best activity. Put "1" beside that activity. The best one will be realistic: It will contribute significantly toward the full accomplishment of the objective; and it will be something you can stay motivated to do. In other words, what one activity from the list will most likely take you the longest distance toward the accomplishment of your objective?

You may also want to select a second best activity, and put "2" beside that activity.

The reason I suggest you not try to do the whole list at once is that I have learned that most people won't follow through on something that complicated and that demanding of their time. But there is no person, of the many I have counseled on this subject, who has not been able to consider adding or changing just one activity in his or her daily life.

In addition, if the objective involves changing an existing habit, that involves mental and emotional resistance. Therefore it is quite difficult to see changes in too many habits at once. Looking at the brighter side, though, if you can see one major improvement in your life become a new habit every six to twelve months, that would amount to a pretty dramatic change over a several-year period. For most of us, the secret to successful personal planning is focusing on priorities, not trying to be overwhelmingly comprehensive. And if, indeed, the objective represents our highest priority desire, there is no other single thing we can do to improve our effectiveness more than to achieve that objective.

As a last helpful hint in this area, let me suggest you write the essence of your planning on a 3x5 card. This would include a summary of your life objective, your six-to-twelve-month objective, and best one or two program activities toward the six-to-twelve-month objective. Then attach the 3x5 card to a corner of your shaving or make-up mirror or to some other place you see every day. This will keep you constantly reminded of your plans.

In conclusion, let me remind you that it is God who gave you the wisdom for these plans and God who empowers you to implement them. Thank Him specifically as you see progress. Now, proceed to the next chapter to see how to work these and other activities into your daily schedule.

4

Scheduling Your Time

In Ephesians 5:15,16, the apostle Paul issues the following warning: " . . . be careful how you walk, not as unwise men, but as wise, making the most of your time, because the days are evil."

How many of us, as we look back over our individual days, feel that we have been making the most of our time? Unfortunately, we often feel we haven't accomplished anything at all.

This frustrating situation often stems from a failure to come to grips with the fact that we live **in time**. This may sound simple, and yet without realizing it, many of us live in the dream world of what we **intend** to do.

Failure of the Listing System Alone

Several years ago while talking with a friend of mine, I asked him how he managed his time; what system did he use? Without comment he pulled out of his desk drawer four sheets of paper. Each of these contained two columns on each side listing the various things my friend wanted to accomplish. To give you an example of what the list contained, one of the items was a major study in the book of Nehemiah.

Now I would guess that a book study of that scope would take many hours to complete, and yet it was just one of dozens, maybe hundreds, of items listed. Not surprisingly, when I asked my friend how his "listing system" worked, he looked embarrassed and replied, "Well, it doesn't."

Now the failure of that system came as no surprise to me—for one simple reason: It had no connection with priorities or time. It was simply a listing of equal priority items with no provision for working these into his day-to-day experience.

In the last chapter, you determined how to implement your number one objective for the next six to twelve months. At this point, the accomplishment of that objective, like my friend's list, is merely a good intention. What you need is a system to translate that intention into action, day by day and week by week, which is where you actually live and do things. Yet at the same time your system needs to provide for your other priority activities.

There are several other good reasons why you should schedule your time. Some of these are scriptural in origin; others are because of the nature of time itself. Let's look first at the scriptural reasons.

The Undisciplined Life Trap

In II Thessalonians 3:11, certain of the Christians in Thessalonica are rebuked for leading undisciplined lives in which nothing of significance is being accomplished. The Thessalonians knew what they should be doing, but their time was somehow being spent on other pursuits.

We as Christians today can fall into the same trap. Unless we actually put into our schedules the activities that we know we should be doing, we will probably end up spending our time on pursuits that will have little significance in the long run.

Time to Do God's Will

In Ecclesiastes 3:1, we learn, "There is an appointed time for everything . . . a time for every event under heaven." There is time to do everything God wants you to do.

We have an example of this in the life of Christ. Jesus' ministry on earth lasted only three and one-half years, and yet He fit into this short span of time all the activities necessary to accomplish God's purpose for Him. "I glorified Thee on earth, having accomplished the work which Thou hast given Me to do" (John 17:4). By focusing on what was important, Jesus accomplished in His brief ministry a more significant mission than any other person in history and launched a worldwide movement that has continued for nearly 2,000 years.

Avoid a Meager Return

In the first chapter of the Book of Haggai, we are shown the results of spending our time on the wrong priorities. Upon their return from captivity, the Israelites had been putting off the building of God's temple in order to first construct luxurious homes for themselves. In order to redirect their attention to Himself, the Lord withheld His blessing in all areas of the Israelites' lives. Consider verse 6:

> You have sown much, but harvest little; you eat, but there is not enough to be satisfied; you drink, but there is not enough to become drunk; you put on clothing, but no one is warm enough; and he who earns, earns wages to put into a purse with holes.

And in verses 10 and 11:

> Therefore, because of you the sky has withheld its dew, and the earth has withheld its produce. And I (the Lord) called for a drought on the land, on the mountains, on the grain, on the new wine, on the oil, on what the ground produces, on men, on cattle, and on all the labor of your hands.

Have you ever had the experience of a very meager return on your investment of time and energy? Perhaps you have been filling your time with the wrong priorities, and God is causing the meager return in order to get your attention. Contrast this with the promise of Matthew 6:33, "But seek first His kingdom, and His righteousness; and all these things shall be added to you."

In addition to these scriptural reasons for scheduling your time, the very nature of time itself demands that you either use it well or lose it.

Time Can't Be Stopped, Stored or Stretched

Did you ever think, for example, about the fact that time cannot be **stopped**? Many of us wish that life were like a game of football in which a team can call "time out" when necessary. We do not have that privilege. Time is perpetually "in"—whether or not we use it wisely.

Just as time cannot be stopped, neither can it be **stored**. In this regard, time might be likened to the manna of the Old Testament. Each morning the Israelites were given just enough of this bread-like substance to last for the day. Some of them tried to save the leftovers only to find that they were filled with worms the following morning. So it is with our time—we must consume it as we get it; what time we waste is gone forever.

Often there is more to do than we can possibly accomplish in the time available, and yet time cannot be **stretched** to include everything.

Overview

In this chapter you will learn how to select and schedule your priority activities from all the possible things you could do with your time. You will have the opportunity to apply these concepts to a short period of time and then to a day. Almost everybody has at least short periods of time during the day in which he can choose which activity to do—even mothers at home with children.

The following are the four steps involved in scheduling your time:

1. List activities.
2. Ask if assignable.
3. Assess priorities.
4. Schedule.

Now, let's take a close look at each of these.

List Activities

Start this step by asking God for His wisdom concerning your activities and schedule. Then list what activities you could do during the period of time you are scheduling. The best way for me to do this is to keep a small sheet of paper with me to list potential activities as they occur to me. As a result my list grows gradually until just before I actually schedule. Then I pray and think more carefully about other potential activities.

Be sure to include in your list the number one priority activity toward your number one objective to accomplish over the next six to twelve months. You should consider this activity for every time period you schedule even though you may not do something concerning it every time. Also include in your list other activities that have been generated by earlier planning efforts. For example, you may have determined a number two priority activity toward your number one objective. Include it on the list. You and your spouse may have talked over supper about some specific things that need to be done soon. Add these to the list.

The following is a checklist of the most frequent categories from which your potential activities will come:

Time with God
Time with family
Time for personal well-being
Life plan
Key items left over from previous day

    Appointments (may already be in schedule)
    Other items from your and other calendars (spouse's,
      secretary's)
    From your plan and/or job description, etc., at work
    Regular commitments
    Letters
    Phone calls
    Items to follow up

This may help you remember all your potential activities.

I have found, though, that sooner or later almost all potential activities surface naturally in our minds. The key point is to capture them in writing in one place, eventually on one sheet of paper.

Ask If Assignable

The next step is to determine if any of the activities on your list are assignable to someone else. Perhaps most of the activities will not be assignable and you must do them yourself. On the other hand, some may be quite possible to assign to other people. Perhaps they could be done better or more appropriately by someone else, or perhaps someone else would simply be willing to do them to free you up for other priorities.

For example, if I need certain facts and statistics to complete a project I am working on, I could do the necessary research myself. However, since there are people on our staff who are especially skilled in this area who could do the research better and faster, I would be wise to ask one of them to help me out in this area.

Or if I need some special type of office supply, I could take the time to find out where to order it and then obtain it myself. It would be very appropriate, however, to ask my secretary to do this. In fact, my secretary relieves me of a number of things that I might otherwise do myself.

Still other activities could be done by someone else simply because he or she would be willing to do them. For example, in my ministry with a number of college students, there were certain events on campus that our group sponsored. I could have done all of the work necessary to set up these events myself. However, the students were very willing and able to do this instead.

When you assign something to someone else, be sure to make clear what you would like him to do. Try to be available to answer his questions as he proceeds. Especially if it is a long assignment, take the initiative to talk to him about the assignment, after a period of time, to see how he is doing.

In conclusion, to do this step, you should consider each activity on your list carefully in terms of its assignability. Then write out the name of the person to whom you are assigning the activity to the left of that activity on the list. Finally, ask the person to do the activity and then follow through to see that it is completed.

Assess Priorities

The next step in the scheduling process is to assess the priorities of the remaining activities. There will always be more things to do than time available. By prioritizing you are determining those things that you want to make sure you do.

To do this, simply put a number one ("1"), number two ("2"), number three ("3"), etc., to the left of each activity according to the priority of its being accomplished in the period of time you are scheduling.

I am often asked what determines priority. This is a good question. Knowing what is priority is really the secret of gaining control of your schedule. There are two key words in prioritizing—importance and urgency. Importance relates to your objectives; urgency relates to time.

An activity is very important to you if it helps you achieve your objectives. It is not very important to you if it does not relate to any of your objectives. Over the long haul, you should, as much as you can, be filling your schedule with important activities.

Let me interject here that you probably have not specifically stated or written down every objective you actually do have. That is not necessarily a problem to prioritizing as long as you can answer the question, "How much does this activity help me accomplish my objectives in life?" A lot? Some? Or very little?

For example, your son may excitedly ask you to attend a baseball game in which, for the first time, he is on the starting team. Encouraging your son helps you accomplish your objectives of loving him and raising him properly. Obviously, this activity is very important for you.

I Thessalonians 5:21 admonishes us to, " . . . examine everything carefully; hold fast to that which is good."

Urgency concerns how soon something must be done. If it can be done anytime in the next six months, it is not very urgent. If it must be done by two hours from now, it is very urgent.

To prioritize is to arrive at one overall rating of the activity in light of its importance and its urgency. If an activity is very important and very urgent, it will probably be your number one priority activity. If another activity is somewhat less important or urgent than this, it may be number two, etc. If an activity is not important and not urgent, it should be far down on your list in terms of priority rating.

Let me warn you that the natural tendency is to pay too much attention to urgency and not enough to importance. If an activity is very urgent but not at all important, you would be wise to give it a fairly low priority. That will probably mean you won't get to it. But, it will also mean that you will have more time for more important activities.

Schedule

The final step in the scheduling process is to actually commit your priority activities to time. More often than not the reason we fail to complete some high priority activities is that we get sidetracked and never get around to spending time on them.

This step insures that the list you have created will actually affect the way you behave. Scheduling is the step in which you really come to grips with the fact that you live in time.

The simplest and most effective way to schedule is to start with your number one priority activity. Block out the time estimated to complete it. Allow for a break, if needed. Enter next your number two priority activity. Block out the time estimated to complete it, etc.

In other words, the first thing you plan to do is your number one priority. When that is done, you then plan to go on to your number two, etc. If by the end of the day you were able to complete only two activities, at least they would be your two highest priorities. What a contrast this is to the common practice of doing all sorts of other activities and never getting to the high priority activities.

Once you have completed your number one priority, number two is the highest priority activity remaining to be done. When it is complete, number three is the highest priority remaining to be done. In other words, you should always seek to do the highest priority activity yet to be done.

Although this idea is simple, I cannot over emphasize the revolutionary impact it can have on your ability to be a good steward of your time before God.

Sample Application of the Four Steps

To illustrate the scheduling of a short block of time, let me share with you a situation that happened to me while giving a week of management training. The day before my "Managing Yourself" talk, a meeting was canceled unexpectedly, giving me two hours of available time. I sat down and scheduled those two hours as follows:

First, I listed the potential activities for these two hours:

Potential activities (as I wrote them)	Explanation of what I meant (I didn't actually write this column. These were just the thoughts in my mind. I try to be brief in what goes down on paper.)
Review talk	Review the "Managing Yourself" talk for tomorrow.
Get overhead projector pens	Obtain a few overhead projector pens for the talk.
Call travel agent	Call the travel agent to straighten out a little complexity on my trip for next week.
Meet with committee	I had been asked to join a committee that afternoon. This was left optional for me.

Second, I asked if each activity was assignable to someone else. I assigned getting the pens to my secretary, Cheryl.

	Review talk
Cheryl	Get overhead projector pens
	Call travel agent
	Meet with the committee

Third, I assessed the priorities of the remaining activities. It was not important for me to attend the committee meeting. The talk and the trip were of equal importance to my long-range objectives, but since the talk was the next day and the trip arrangements could wait, I wrote down the following:

	1.	Review talk
Cheryl		Get overhead projector pens
	2.	Call travel agent
	3.	Meet with committee

Fourth, I called Cheryl on the intercom and asked her to get the pens. Then I scheduled the review of the talk to take the next 1½ hours and calling the travel agent to take the last half hour.

The review took the whole two hours available, so I had to call the travel agent the next day and did not attend the committee meeting. However, when the two hours were over, I felt assured that my time had been invested in the best possible way. I could have spent the whole two hours looking for some pens or meeting with the committee and not gotten to the more important matter of reviewing the talk.

Now It's Your Turn

Now I would like for you to schedule a two-to-three-hour block of your own time. Select a time, preferably within the next 24 hours, which you are free to spend as you choose. Pick a time during which you would not normally be sleeping or eating or would not otherwise be doing just one kind of activity.

When you have that time in mind, you are ready to schedule it, just as in the example. Take out a sheet of paper and, first, prayerfully list the activities that you could do in that time. Next, ask if any of them are assignable. Then, assess the priorities of the remaining activities. Finally, work out a tentative schedule by simply writing an estimated time for completion to the right of each activity. Pause here and apply this outline.

Some Refinements in Your Scheduling

The following are a few refinements that will help the simple scheduling process to be most useful to you.

First, you need to determine what length of time you are going to schedule. Some people's schedules are so unpredictable that they are wisest simply to keep their prioritized list with them. When they have some discretionary time, they should start doing their number one priority. If they complete it, they should go on to number two, etc. Secretaries and mothers of young children are two groups of people who are commonly in the position of having frequent demands placed on their time by someone else.

Most people, though, can look ahead to the next day with some certainty. I recommend that you schedule at least a large segment of a day at a time if possible. If you do this the night before, you will be able to set your mind at ease that you aren't going to forget to do something important, and you will wake up in the morning ready to get started making the most of that day.

Some people find it almost a necessity to schedule more into the future than one day at a time. Especially for such people, Chapter 10 in Part II of this book gives more detail.

A second refinement has to do with which activities to prioritize and schedule versus some that you may simply wish to view as standard and, therefore, already scheduled. In scheduling a day, for example, it simplifies things to place into your schedule first the very basic activities of the day, such as: time to wake up, bathroom time, devotions, breakfast, travel to work, lunch, travel home, dinner, and time to go to bed. There may be other standard activities customed to you such as: getting the children ready for school, attending the department meeting every morning from 8 to 8:30, etc. These activities break up the day into a series of blocks of time in which you have a choice as to what to do and into which you can place your activities in order of priority. Occasionally you should evaluate the real priority of these standard items to be sure they deserve the time you are giving them.

Third, it may be that your number one priority activity can't be done immediately. Perhaps it is an appointment for later in the day (or whatever block of time you are scheduling). All you can do is schedule it when it should occur and don't schedule before it an activity that often runs long.

A fourth refinement has to do with the time needed for the activities you are scheduling. If you schedule one day at a time and you project your number one activity to take

30 hours to complete, the above schedule procedure would lead you to block every available hour in the day. This may be appropriate, but normally I find it is better to break up long activities into one-to-three-hour bite-sized pieces. That is the typical length of time most people can spend on one activity before they need a break. (The planning outline mentioned in Chapter 3 and detailed more in Chapter 8 will be of help to you in thinking through major projects to the point of having smaller activities.) You may find that the first bite-sized piece is indeed your number one priority. The next piece may not be number two in light of other activities which should be done during that day. (You may have a few critical phone calls to make, for example.)

A fifth refinement has to do with maintaining your motivation at a high level. Often a few activities on your list are very high priority because you don't like to do them and have been putting them off. If you schedule several of these in a row on one day, you may find it virtually impossible to look forward to the day. One solution to this I use is to schedule something I particularly like to do as a "reward" right after completing something that I don't naturally like to do. (In Chapter 5 you will find some additional suggested ways to handle the "disliked" activities.)

Sixth, learn to be realistic about logical time to engage in certain kinds of activities. Most people are more alert from 9-11 in the morning than they are from 1-3 in the afternoon. Therefore, for most people it is better to schedule activities demanding high creativity in the 9-11 slot and activities that are more routine in the 1-3 slot.

Seventh, for many people time available to be scheduled in a day falls into two major categories: at work during the day and at home during the evening. For the most part, any given activity would most naturally be done in only one of the two places. A business meeting would normally occur at the office, whereas time with the children would normally occur at home. As a result I find it is more realistic for such people to create two lists for their potential activities for the day, one for work and one for home. They then assign, prioritize and schedule the lists separately.

Example of Scheduling a Day

The following is an illustration of a person scheduling a day using the four steps and some of the refinements.

First, he prayerfully listed his activities. He had previously found that the time over which he exercised choice fell into two large pieces: at the office during the day and at home in the evening. Therefore he actually listed, assigned, prioritized and scheduled at two different times. He worked on the "office" schedule just before he left the office the previous day. He worked on the home schedule before he went to bed the night previous to the evening being scheduled.

Normally a portion of his waking hours were spent in pretty much of a standard way: wake-up at 6 a.m.; bathroom and dressing time, 6-6:30; personal devotions, 6:30-7; breakfast, 7-7:30; travel to work, 7:30-8; lunch, 12-1; travel home, 5:30-6; supper, 6-7; bedtime, 10:30.

In addition to his standard time "commitments," he had one appointment already scheduled for the day. It was an interview with a job candidate from 2-3:30. He viewed this as already committed time.

In order to schedule his remaining time during the day and evening, he created the following two lists:

OFFICE

Prepare report on new products project
Review efficiency study on my department
Make important phone calls (Chuck, Warren and Chris)
Follow up on order from Green Products
Read trade magazines
Do correspondence
Share Christ with George over lunch
Tour department and meet briefly with each supervisor
Gather information for forthcoming department meeting

HOME

Go shopping with Jane
Call men on next week's Bible study
Walk for exercise (Note: This was his number one activity
                 toward his number one objective.)
Relax and read

Second, with each list he asked if each activity was assign-able. He determined to assign the follow-up on the order to Vicki, his secretary, and the gathering of information to Dave, one of the supervisors in the department.

Third, with each list he assessed the priority of each of the remaining activities. Sharing Christ with George was both important and urgent due to the fact George was leaving the department the next week. Certain phone calls were also very high priority, etc. The following is how the lists looked after asking if assignable and assessing priorities:

OFFICE

3	Prepare report on new products project
6	Review efficiency study on my department
2	Make important phone calls (Chuck, Warren and Chris)
Vicki	Follow up on order from Green Products
7	Read trade magazines
5	Do correspondence
1	Share Christ with George over lunch
4	Tour department and meet briefly with each supervisor
Dave	Gather information for forthcoming department meeting

HOME

4	Go shopping with Jane
1	Call men on next week's Bible study
3	Walk for exercise
2	Relax

Fourth, he entered his activities into his schedule. For each of the two major parts of his day he entered his number one priority first, then number two, etc., until there was no longer time realistically available. The following is what his office and home schedules finally looked like:

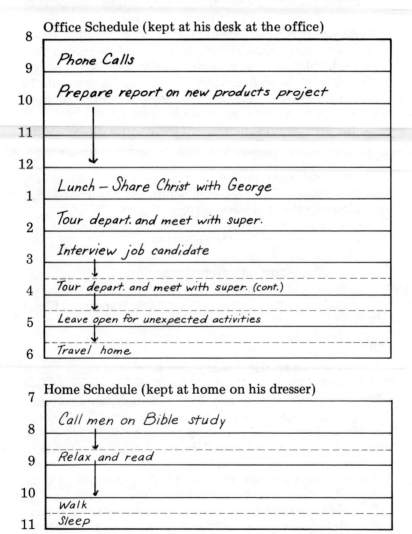

Office Schedule (kept at his desk at the office)

8	
9	*Phone Calls*
10	*Prepare report on new products project*
11	
12	
1	*Lunch – Share Christ with George*
2	*Tour depart. and meet with super.*
3	*Interview job candidate*
4	*Tour depart. and meet with super. (cont.)*
5	*Leave open for unexpected activities*
6	*Travel home*

Home Schedule (kept at home on his dresser)

7	
8	*Call men on Bible study*
9	*Relax and read*
10	
	Walk
11	*Sleep*

Your Turn Again

Now that you have considered the example, I would like for you to schedule a day of your own time. Why not begin with tomorrow? Or, if you are reading this book first thing in the morning, you can schedule the rest of today.

If the short block of time that you have already scheduled is within the day you select, then just schedule around that time, since there is no need to schedule it again.

When you have chosen a day to schedule, you are ready to proceed. As in the example, begin with prayer and then quickly list on a clean sheet of paper the activities that you could spend your time on. Don't forget to include in your list the number one activity toward your number one objective.

Second, determine if any of the activities are assignable, making notations as appropriate. Third, number the remaining activities according to priority.

Fourth, schedule your activities, in order of priority. Although for this application you can make a schedule like the one in the example, for future scheduling you might take advantage of the various daily schedule sheets that are available at most office supply outlets and in some department stores.

Conclusion

Congratulations! You have now learned and applied how to schedule your time. If you will do this every day, I can assure you that it will be one of the best habits you will ever start. It will go far in helping you make the most of your time as Paul urged us all to do in Ephesians 5:15,16. It will enable you to look back over your days with the satisfaction of knowing you have really accomplished the priority activities and are actually moving toward the achievement of your objectives.

Now this is assuming, of course, that you actually **follow** the schedule you have planned. Perhaps for you, as for many,

this is easier said than done. In the next chapter you will
learn how to follow through on what you have determined
to do.

5

Following Your Schedule

I have seen some outstanding plans and some equally impressive schedules which did not benefit their authors in the least, for one simple reason: They were never implemented. How often we intend to do something, even to the point of writing it down, and then fail to follow through. If that happens, the time we have spent planning and scheduling is wasted, and our likelihood of doing what God has shown us is greatly diminished.

In II Corinthians, we are given a prime scriptural example of unfulfilled intentions. In this situation the church at Corinth has been intending for some time to finish raising a sum of money for the needs of the saints, but they have not yet done it. In II Corinthians 8:10,11, Paul admonishes them as follows: "I want to suggest that you finish what you started to do a year ago, . . . Having started the ball rolling so enthusiastically, you should carry this project through to completion just as gladly, . . . Let your enthusiastic idea at the start be equalled by your realistic action now" (Living Bible).

The purpose of this chapter is to help you follow through

and yet stay relaxed and sensitive. I would like to share with you four principles which I have found invaluable: motivation, discipline, sensitivity and peace. These principles are not "how to's" in the sense that they can be followed in a "step one, step two, etc." manner, but rather are general concepts from which you can draw as you proceed through your day. To show you how this is done, I will end the chapter with an example of how one particular person applied these concepts in his own situation.

Motivation Is the Key

In Philippians 2:13 we are told: "For it is God who is at work in you, both to will and to work for His good pleasure." To paraphrase a little, that means that God is able to work inside of us to change our desires. Probably the greatest key I can give you in the area of following your schedule is to let God cause you to be motivated correctly.

If we like to do something, we tend to do it. Usually we have an opinion on any given activity. We either like to do it or we don't like to do it. The activities we like to do we might call "ice cream" activities. Those we don't like to do we could call "liver" activities. I love ice cream, and I am not naturally fond of liver. If ice cream were only as good for me as liver is, I would find it very easy to be healthy.

Now if all I had to do all day long were my "ice cream" activities, I would have no problem, because I find I am really anxious to do them any time of the day. On the other hand, I tend to put off the "liver" activities with almost any excuse, even though in most cases I eventually must do them. I used to find that I would have quite a list of "liver" activities undone at the end of the day simply because my discipline was not sufficient to compensate for my distaste.

It eventually occurred to me that my days would be more interesting and productive if I did only what I enjoyed. That left me with the alternatives of becoming undependable relative to the "liver" activities or of learning to like the previously unliked. That is when the powerful truth of Philippians 2:13 broke through to me. God can change my likes and dislikes! I just needed to ask and trust Him.

I often ask audiences, "How many of you enjoyed studying the Bible before you became a Christian?" Nobody responds. Then I ask, "How many enjoy studying the Bible now, after you have become a Christian?" Many, if not almost all, respond "yes." Why? Because God has been at work in their lives changing their desires.

The same was true in my own life. I now like to study the Bible, because God changed my desires. God has also changed my desires about other activities. I now like to do many things that I previously found very dull.

Surely you, too, face certain activites that you don't like but that you must do. So long as the activity is consistent with God's will, you can pray for a genuine enthusiasm and then step out in faith, counting on a change of heart toward the activity.

Remember, God has commanded us to do everything joyfully (Philippians 4:4-7), and He would never ask us to do this if He were not also willing to make that joy possible.

Just think how pleasant your days would be if you trusted God to make all that you had to do enjoyable. I have personally found that at the end of such days, I feel as refreshed as I did at the beginning of the day.

Motivation Involves Keeping the Goal in Sight

Another source of motivation for activities is to keep steadily before you the reasons you are doing them. As you recall the long-range benefits of your activities, the inconvenience of the short-range will not loom so large.

For example, have you ever known a young lady who is having a problem with her weight to put the picture of a slim model in a skimpy bathing suit just above the handle of the refrigerator door? When she is tempted to snack, she is reminded of why she should not give in, and as she eyes that picture of what she eventually might look like, it becomes easier to walk away empty-handed.

I have often thought that a good refinement of this strategy would be to put a picture of a very heavy, bikini-clad woman on the **inside** of the refrigerator with the caption, "Now that you've arrived."

In my own office, I keep on display two large maps of the world. These serve to remind me that the ultimate purpose of all that I am doing is to help reach that world for Christ. Sometimes when I'm doing dictation or other kinds of paper work that are not naturally interesting to me, I'm reminded by a glance at these maps that what I am doing has a very worthwhile and desirable purpose, and I am inspired to go on.

You may want to use symbols or meaningful pictures yourself to help remind you why you are doing the tasks that you do not naturally enjoy. These reminders may really help you to keep going when your enthusiasm for a particular activity begins to lag.

Discipline Available to All

The second ingredient in successful schedule-following is discipline. Some of us, it seems, come by this useful trait almost naturally, but for those of us who don't, following through on our plans can be a real battle.

Fortunately for us, we can win that battle, for the ninth part of the fruit of the Spirit is self-control. As mentioned in Chapter 1, the Greek word that translates as "self-control" literally means "controlling power" or the ability to be under control. As we grow and mature as Christians, this ability should characterize our lives more and more.

The question is, how can we appropriate this discipline or self-control as Christians right now? The answer is found in I John 5:14,15: "And this is the confidence which we have before Him, that, if we ask anything according to His will, He hears us. And if we know that He hears us in whatever we ask, we know that we have the requests which we have asked from Him."

From this verse we learn that there are two conditions

which must exist in order for us to obtain our requests from the Lord. The first is that the object of our desire be consistent with God's will for our lives; the second is that we actually take the time to ask Him for what we want, believing that He will answer our prayers.

Do you, in fact, believe that it is God's will that you exercise discipline in following through on the plans that you have made under His guidance? Certainly it is, or He would not have promised you the needed self-control. It remains, then, for you to ask God in faith for what you need, believing that He will bring about a work of discipline in your life.

Discipline for Specific Situations

I remember teaching this subject in a Sunday school class in which two of the members were former alcoholics. When I got to the part about the Lord supplying self-control when we cannot come up with it in our own strength, both of them nodded their heads in firm agreement. In their particular cases, the self-control was applied to abstaining from alcohol, but this same discipline can be applied to any situation where it is needed to accomplish God's will.

In my own life, I have found that I need a special measure of discipline when getting started on a new project. Therefore, when I must begin something new, I ask God to give me the resolve, and then I step out in faith and begin. Generally, the project seems to become easier as I proceed.

I once heard a talk by a very successful businessman who claimed that the best way to actually get into an activity was to begin it. This particular fellow lives on Lake Michigan and he found that the only way he could begin swimming in that very cold water was simply to plunge in. Wading in until the water was up to his neck didn't work. He called his technique the "plunge" approach. God can provide the discipline needed to take the plunge into whatever it is that **you** must do.

I also find that I need discipline to keep me going once

a project is started, particularly when it is a long one. Putting together this book, for example, took a long time, and it was only by a special measure of God's discipline that I was able to keep at it until the end. The Corinthians apparently had the same need, for as we saw, Paul had to encourage them to fully complete what they set out to do.

I am sure you have found this situation true in your own experience—you simply run out of gas after awhile, and an extra measure of discipline is needed to get you going again. This is particularly true of most people when a project is substantially completed, but not really done as it should be. Again, you can rely on the Lord to supply the discipline needed to see you through. Simply ask in faith, then act as evidence of your faith. "Even so faith, if it has no works, is dead, being by itself" (James 2:17).

Sensitivity to God and to People

The third ingredient in effective schedule-following is a sensitivity to God's leading and to people's needs.

In John 10:27, Jesus says, "My sheep hear My voice, and I know them, and they follow Me." In whatever we do, whether we are following a schedule or not, we need to be sensitive to God's leading at all times.

When we become very well-planned and well-scheduled, it is sometimes easy to dull our senses to God. Sometimes God uses our plans to get us in a position from which He can direct us to something unexpected that He would like us to do. But if we are so locked into our own plans that we are not receptive to God at these times, then we miss what He has for us.

In the example at the end of the chapter we will see some specific ways to handle the interruptions that normally occur in the course of a day. The principle to remember here, however, is simply to remain sensitive at all times to the impressions that God might send. Let's not forget that it is God's ultimate, refined plan that we want for our lives, whereas the schedule that is before us is really only the first draft of that plan.

The caution here, of course, is to realize that God is not the only source of impressions. Sometimes we need to test our impressions to be sure that they are from the Lord and not from ourselves or from Satan.

I find that the best way to handle impressions is first to make sure that I am always walking in the Spirit. Then, when I am impressed to veer from my schedule in some way, I simply pray and ask God to confirm that the impression is really from Him. I am especially suspicious when a new impression is totally contrary to several of the things I felt impressed of God to do when I came up with my schedule in the first place.

In I Corinthians 13:1-3 we find that, if we speak with angelic tongues, prophesy, know all, have all faith, give away our possessions and even our lives, and do not have love, we have utterly failed in life. I would add that, if we religiously follow our schedules in such a way that we are insensitive to or even offend the people around us, we have also failed.

We see an instructive example of Jesus' purposefulness and sensitivity in balance in Matthew 14. Jesus had just heard of John the Baptist's death and wanted to be by Himself to pray. The multitudes, however, pressed to see Him and be healed. Jesus felt compassion and changed His plans. He healed them and fed them miraculously. Then He made the disciples travel on ahead of Him and sent the multitude away. Finally He retreated to the mountain to pray alone, as was His original intention.

The Peace of God

In Philippians 4:7 we are promised " . . . the peace of God, which surpasses all comprehension, shall guard your hearts and your minds in Christ Jesus." The fourth and final ingredient in the successful following of a schedule is the kind of peace that only God can supply.

Most of us can be pressured to the point that we eventually become less effective. We all tend to get under the pile and become discouraged by circumstances, particularly when we have an overload of work.

In whatever circumstance you find yourself, whether you are facing problems with your schedule or in other areas, realize that peace, like discipline or self-control, is a part of the fruit of the Spirit and can be appropriated by faith in the same manner.

Through His own life, Jesus gives us an example of the peace which is not based on circumstances. Just before He was to die, we see Jesus calmly telling the Father in John 17:4 that He (Jesus) had glorified the Father on earth and had done everything that was asked of Him.

Now here was a person who had come to earth expressly to "seek and to save that which was lost," and on the eve of His death He knew that many people in the world were still lost. And yet Jesus was at peace for He realized that He had done everything He had been asked to do in His earthly ministry.

That same peace should characterize our own lives as Christians. If we are praying and asking God to reveal the priorities that should be filling our days, and if we are, in fact, doing our best to follow through on these and are at the same time trusting God to make us sensitive to any changes He would have us make in our plans, then there is no reason we should be upset with the things that don't get done.

We can only do so many things in the hours God has given us; and if we do the things He has asked us to do, then, like Jesus, we can know that we have glorified Him, and we can experience peace.

If for some reason you are lacking that peace, pray and ask God to give you a special measure to help you overcome whatever circumstances you might face, whatever activities are yet to be done, no matter how pressing they may seem. You will be much more effective at facing the problems of the day if you approach them in a calm, tension-free frame of mind.

Some people I know even have trouble going to sleep at

night because of all the things they have to do. I keep a pad of paper near my bed. When a problem begins to occupy my mind at night, I write it down and ask God to take away any anxiety I might have. I Peter 5:7 tells us we should be "casting all your anxiety upon Him, because He cares for you." Then I praise and thank God for His provision on this. Then at times I mentally sing some familiar song of praise to God, thus filling my mind with God instead of the problem, which is what we are commanded to do in Philippians 4:4-8.

Example

We have now examined four key concepts that relate to following a schedule successfully. These concepts—motivation, discipline, sensitivity and peace—will help you follow what you have scheduled without becoming a "robot" and without becoming filled with anxiety. They will help you realize your objectives in a way that will bring glory to God and a deep sense of satisfaction to you.

To illustrate further how these concepts can relate to your daily life, I would like now to take you through a day in the life of a person applying these concepts:

John has a busy day ahead of him. He is working on the promotion and arrangements for a management training seminar for 150 to 200 Christian people, in addition to his normal schedule of meetings, letters and projects. However, the seminar has become a very high priority as it draws nearer and the total number of registrations is lower than expected.

A new group of potential attendees has been selected for a mailing and the previously contacted people need to be followed up to encourage attendance. John is a slow mover in the morning and arrives at work a few minutes late. He has experienced some personal frustrations lately and his mind wanders from his job occasionally.

John, however, knows the resources that are available to him through his personal relationship with Christ. He immediately pauses at his desk to ask God for necessary wisdom and motivation to make him effective in his work. God has been very faithful in providing His promised motiva-tion and discipline whenever John has requested His help. Today, John specifically asks God to allow him to enjoy the work for which he is responsible, for he knows he is much more highly motivated when he enjoys the work he is doing. As he prays, John reminds himself of how the seminar will contribute to the goals of his organization and how it will build leadership and management skills into the individuals who attend. He reminds himself of the benefits that will be derived for everyone concerned.

John is excited about what he needs to do, but now he can't seem to take that first step to write the new promo-tional letter. Then he remembers that self-control is one part of the fruit of the Spirit, so he prays for discipline, picks up the pencil and begins to write, asking God to pro-vide the needed wisdom.

The letter and registration form are finished, but must be typed and printed. As John leaves his office to take the letter to his secretary, his boss calls him in to assign a new project, which must be completed by the end of the week. John is momentarily frustrated, but he remembers that God has placed his boss in a position of authority over him, realizing that the new assignment is part of God's will for his life.

When John reaches his secretary, he explains the letter and information to be typed and printed. His secretary in-forms him that three people have called and requested that he call back: his wife, a friend from out-of-town and a pastor requesting information about the seminar. However, John's first appointment, Mr. Smith, is waiting for his scheduled meeting.

John quickly asks God for wisdom. He asks his secretary to take Mr. Smith into his office and fix him some coffee while he briefly calls home. John's wife is concerned about the hot water heater, and John is able to remember whom she should call to fix it.

The day doesn't get any easier. John personally needs to

call 30 pastors to follow up his letter concerning the management training seminar. As pressures build during the day, and the projects appear larger than the time available, frustration and worry begin to close in on John. He wants to be a faithful steward, but the responsibilities seem impossible.

At this time, John prays again, asking God for His promised peace, and remembers God's magnificent character. His God is not a God who loses control of anything. He knows his every need, including his time schedule. He is a God who is constantly concerned for him.

John stays a little later than he expected, but he finally determines that he has done all that he can for the day. John determines to relax and trust God for the final results of his efforts, and he heads for home.

Life can get very busy at times. God stands ready and able to give us motivation, discipline, sensitivity and peace. All we need to do is ask Him and step out in faith.

Before leaving this chapter, select one of the four principles presented which most helps you in an area of need. Think of specific ways you can apply the principles within the next day or two. Pray and ask God to help you follow through.

6

Multiplying Your Time

Several years ago, I attended a training seminar at Purdue University. It was the first time in a long while that I had been in a dorm type of living situation.

The very first morning when I woke up, I slipped quietly out of the room so as not to awaken my roommate, went all the way down the hall to the shower and bathrooms, got ready for my shower and then, just as I was ready to step in, I discovered that I did not have my shampoo with me. At home my shampoo was already in the bathroom. I walked all the way back down the hall to my room, quietly slipped in and got my shampoo, went all the way back, got ready to shower and discovered I did not have my towel. At home my towel was kept along side the shower.

Well, I went all the way back to the room and got my towel, came back to the shower room, and as I was finally taking my shower, it occurred to me that there was probably a better way! Tomorrow I would try to remember to bring everything with me in the first place.

Perhaps you have had a similar experience yourself. Have you completed a project and then realized that it could have been done another way in half the time? Have you ever gotten all the way back from a shopping trip downtown only to realize that you should have picked up something else while you were there? Have you worked alongside someone in a volunteer situation and noticed that he had a knack for accomplishing the task very quickly and efficiently?

Multiply Your Time

Moment by moment we are all faced with opportunities to multiply our time so that we are more effective. Sometimes this is accomplished by doing two things at once, such as listening to a tape while driving to work. Other times, it is simply a matter of thinking carefully about the one thing we are doing so that we do that job in the best possible way. At any rate, when we multiply our time, we accomplish the most possible with each moment that we have, and we make each activity count to the fullest.

What Do the Scriptures Say?

The Scriptures encourage us to be effective and efficient. Do you remember, for example, the parable of the talents from Matthew 25 that we discussed in Chapter 1? God expects us to see a good return on the resources He gives us to invest.

Concerning the subject of waste, consider the feeding of the 5,000 as recounted in Mark 6:35-44. In verse 43 it is recorded that, when everyone had finished eating, the disciples picked up 12 full baskets of leftovers. We see a similar situation in the feeding of the 4,000: "And they ate and were satisfied; and they picked up seven full baskets of what was left over of the broken pieces" (Mark 8:8). In Mark 8:19,20 Jesus reminds the disciples of the exact number of baskets of leftovers in both cases.

Christ had performed two great miracles, creating food beyond the hunger of even the large crowds. But instead of the extra being thrown away, it was carefully stored for future use. Furthermore, the Scriptures record and reiterate the precise leftover inventory. It appears to me that God has placed before us a real example of how we should not be wasteful.

In Colossians 4:2-6 we also see an emphasis on being effective in what we do:

> Devote yourselves to prayer, keeping alert in it with an attitude of thanksgiving; praying at the same time for us as well, that God may open up to us a door for the word, so that we may speak forth the mystery of Christ, for which I also have been imprisoned; in order that I may make it clear in the way I ought to speak. Conduct yourselves with wisdom toward outsiders, making the most of the opportunity. Let your speech always be with grace, seasoned, as it were, with salt, so that you may know how you should respond to each person.

The Colossians were to pray with devotion and alertness versus lazily and sleepily. They were to do two things at once: have an attitude of thanksgiving and pray for Paul and his companions. Paul wanted to be clear in his speech. The Colossians were to wisely make the most of their interaction with outsiders, speaking and responding sensitively and with carefully chosen words.

There seems to be a real message to us here: to do things well. This is reinforced by I Corinthians 10:31, " . . . whatever you do, do all to the glory of God."

God's Wisdom Is Available

Since it is God's will that we make the best use of our time, He is also graciously willing to provide us with the wisdom to do so. In Proverbs 2:7 we are told that God "stores up sound wisdom for the upright"; and in I Corinthians 2:16, we are told that as Christians we have the mind of Christ.

Therefore, if you are stumped as to how to do something

most effectively, remember that you always have free access to God to ask Him for guidance.

In the remainder of this chapter, I would like to share with you some ideas and methods that have been of great help to me as I have sought to increase my own effectiveness. First, I would like to show you how you can begin to think **generally** about multiplying your time, and then I will be giving you some very **specific** hints as to how you can become more multiplied in a number of different situations. The advantage of learning a general approach is that you can then face a wide variety of circumstances and yet adapt and see rapid improvement in your effectiveness.

A General Approach

Do you recall the how-to-plan outline mentioned in Chapter 3? It contains five steps: pray, establish objectives, program, schedule and budget. There are many specific questions I ask myself to test for maximum effectiveness in any situation. In summary, though, they basically are testing to see if there is a good plan being used. The following are representative of the thoughts that can help you maximize your effectiveness:

Pray

Have you prayed? Were you specific? Do some Scriptures come to mind? Do any other ideas come to mind after prayer? Is it appropriate for others to join in prayer for this? How can you encourage that? Do you have any sense that you are basically trusting in your own strength and not in God's power to accomplish this project? Be sure to pray and ask God for His wisdom and enablement.

Establish Objectives

Why are you doing this project? What are you trying to accomplish? Be precise; don't include unintended extras in your description of what you are trying to accomplish. Is it getting you closer to the objectives that you have determined for yourself, your family or your job? If not, are you for some other reason constrained to do this? If not, why are you doing it? What would happen if you didn't even do it? If nothing significant would happen, consider not doing it at all.

Is the objective of the project clear to everyone who is working on it? If not, can you help clarify it? Other than prayer, the single most important contributor to success on a project is a clearly defined, well-understood objective.

The most frequent question I ask in meetings is, "What is our objective?" More often than not it has not been defined or has not been revealed to the group, making progress difficult at best. I want my contribution to a meeting to be helpful and positive, but that is difficult without knowing the objective. In fact, it is very difficult to take good notes on and comment on a presentation unless I know the objective of the presentation and the objective of my participation. Am I just to be informed or am I to help improve the item being discussed?

Be aggressive in seeking to know what you hope to accomplish in everything you do.

Program

Is what you are doing contributing to the objective significantly? If not, how can you alter your activities to contribute? Are the others around you contributing well to the objective? If not, is there anything you can do to help them?

How are you doing what you are doing? Do you need to do everything that you are doing in order to accomplish the objective? Look at each step and ask if it is necessary. If that doesn't improve things, try looking at it another way: What one thing can you do to get the maximum distance toward the objective? Why not start by just doing that? Then ask what additional things are needed to further accomplish the objective. As a rule, the fewer number of activities that are needed to accomplish the objective, the better.

Would it cut down the time and effort needed to do what you are doing if you change the position or layout of the various elements?

Does your activity utilize you doing something you do naturally or at least like to do? If not, can it possibly involve something you enjoy doing and/or do well?

Have you ever seen this activity, or one that is similar, done before? How was it done? Can you think of any hints from what you saw before as to how you could do the activity better? By the way, it is a good idea to learn to observe carefully and to be inquisitive about everything you see. Ask yourself often, "I wonder why that is done in such a way?" Think about it awhile before you ask anyone; but then do feel free to ask when the moment is right. One of the unfortunate things about growing up is that we lose our childlike curiosity and willingness to ask questions.

Do you know anyone who might know more about your activity than you do? If so, ask him how you might become better at it. Of course, we need to be sensitive not to impose on others, but I have found that most people like to talk about their areas of expertise.

Do you know of a book or an article or of some other source of information that relates to what you are doing? If so, see if you can obtain it and then look over the section that pertains to what you are doing. Be very careful not to get too tied up in all the other sections unless they pertain to other things you want to do. For me one of the easiest ways to procrastinate is to idly read or leaf through a magazine or book.

If you learn better by trying something, how can you practice without ruining the final outcome of the project?

As you seek to improve the way you do the activity, question anything related to it that looks like a tradition or an assumption. This practice may very well reveal a better approach for you. Some time ago, for example, I asked myself why most people work sitting at a desk. I went on to question that practice as it related to my own situation, and my line of thinking went something like this: What am I really trying to accomplish? At my desk, I am primarily trying to do think-work. What is the most crucial ingredient in think-work? Alertness! What does a comfortable chair do to me, especially after lunch? It makes me sleepy. Therefore, I either need to have an uncomfortable chair at my desk, or perhaps even better, I could stand up to work.

As a result of simply questioning a tradition, I now do think-work at a stand-up desk; and I find that it does vastly improve my alertness.

Another assumption I once challenged is that we should look at only one sheet of paper at a time as we work. On one hand, this procedure has certain benefits in that we don't want to be distracted by material that does not relate to what we are doing. On the other hand, I have found that by spreading out many different sheets of paper that all relate to the same subject, I can better conceptualize talks or writing projects or whatever it is I must do. The reason is that, as I am able to scan a number of different facts at the same time and fill my brain with them, I can better tie those facts together.

In summary, all of the questions in this "program" section are intended to test and improve the effectiveness of your activities in accomplishing your objectives.

Schedule

Do you know when the different parts of your plan must be done? Are these deadlines before you as you schedule your time day by day? Are the other people involved aware of when they need to complete their parts? Do you have evidence that they are going to be done on time?

If it looks as though you and/or others are not going to be done on time and if timing is critical, do you have an alternative plan?

Is your schedule on this project compatible with other things you must do? If you will probably be overloaded in any given time period in the future, can you reschedule any of your activities to avoid a totally unrealistic plan?

Is your schedule realistic in terms of your energy cycle during the day? If it calls on you to do the most creative parts of the project at a time when you are normally not at your peak alertness, can you change that aspect of the schedule?

Do you have any past experience with how long your planned activities tend to take? Are you being realistic in light of that, with some stretch built in so you can try to improve on your past effectiveness?

Are there any immediate partial accomplishment targets that you can set for yourself? These will allow you to experience some quick indications of progress.

Have you ever heard of the 80/20 rule? It states that most often 80% of your objective is accomplished by the first 20% of your time spent and that the remaining 20% of your objective is accomplished by the subsequent 80% of your time on the project. In light of that, you need to really ask yourself if the remaining 20% of the objective is worth the further investment of your time. If it is, great! If not, you have just saved yourself a lot of time.

Budget

Have you determined what resources will be needed for the project? Carefully think through each activity to completion. Have you considered every material and facility that is needed? Do you need help at any juncture? How much money is needed?

Where are you obtaining these resources? Do you know where to obtain them at the best price? Use the phone rather than your car to price things.

Have you prayed and asked God for any special provision He may have for you? Several times I have prayed for an item, and within a day or two a person has walked in the door with it in his hands, seeking to give it away. By the way, if you have more than you need of some resource, be sensitive to the needs others around you may have. God frequently gives us a surplus so we can experience the joy of giving.

In summary, this is the general approach I use to try to make the most of my time as I do things. When you are getting ready to start something, reread this section. Ask yourself some of these questions during the next meeting you attend, and be sure to reread the section carefully before planning the next meeting for which you are responsible. More than anything else, become more aggressive in your thinking relative to what you do. Don't initially accept the way you have always done something as the best way to do it. Strive for excellence in your activities, with a freedom from waste.

Some Specific Helpful Hints

The following are some specific ideas on how to multiply your time in a number of kinds of situations.

1. Job or ministry.
    a. Force yourself to make decisions. Don't just stare at a blank sheet of paper. Set a deadline for a decision, if more thinking is needed.
    b. Learn to say "no" to others and to yourself. Don't get involved in activities you don't have time to do.
    c. Delegate everything you can. Don't overlook volunteer workers. Be sure to give adequate instructions, or it may take more of your time to redo the task later.
    d. Look for outdated or otherwise unneeded procedures.
    e. Maintain a good system for recording and reminding yourself of the things you need to do in the future. Use a pocket or purse calendar which has a small space for each day for at least several months to come. Check this before committing to future plans. Reference this when scheduling your day.
    f. Maintain a good overall filing system. This means less time looking for misplaced items. One of the best ways to organize your filing system is according to the activities in your plan or to the responsibilities

in your job description.

g. To think of more time-saving ideas, brainstorm with others who have jobs similar to yours or who are in similar situations. This is a good habit to make part of your lifestyle.

h. Use your time twice. Listen to tapes while doing mechanical work. Look for work that can be done if there are dead times in large meetings.

2. Typical time wasters.

a. Sleeping too much. By all means get what sleep you really need for health and alertness. But here is an area where many people really indulge themselves with little return on the time invested. Try a little less sleep at night and a nap during the day, if that is possible. That sometimes results in fewer hours total sleep, but more alertness during the day.

b. Watching too much television. Have you ever heard "The 23rd Channel"? It goes like this:

> The TV is my shepherd.
> It maketh me to sit down and
> Do nothing for His Name's sake,
> Because it requireth all
> My spare time.
>
> It restoreth my knowledge of
> The things of the world,
> And keepeth me from the
> Study of God's Word.
> Its sound and picture
> They comfort me.
>
> Yea, though I live to be 100,
> I shall keep on viewing
> As long as it works.
> Surely no good thing
> Will come of my life.
>
> Author Unknown

    c. Not planning evenings.

    d. Talking too long with friends. It certainly isn't wrong to talk to your friends, but some people do far too much of that and too little of other worthy pursuits.

    e. Thumbing through magazines.

    f. Chronic visiting in the office.

3. Travel.

    a. Use your travel time to get things done. Listen to tapes, dictate letters, catch up on "must" reading, prepare for upcoming meetings, etc.

    b. When you are flying into a city for a short meeting, consider holding it at the air terminal when possible.

    c. Don't drive during rush hours.

    d. Keep your car in good mechanical condition. Breakdowns may cost you hours (as well as dollars), plus they will probably cause you to miss your scheduled activity.

    e. Plan your errands. Avoid traveling back and forth across town. Try to think ahead about things you will need the next day or two and pick them up on this trip if possible. Avoid numerous trips per day back and forth between your home and where you work. Remember, if you don't use your head, you will have to use your feet instead.

4. Thinking.

    a. Allow from one to three hours of uninterrupted time for think work (preparing talks, etc.).

    b. Go some place where no one will bother you.

    c. Work when the other people in the house are asleep (early in the morning or late at night).

    d. Come to the office an hour early or stay an hour late.

    e. Be sure to include think time as a specific item in your schedule rather than waiting for free time.

    f. Have other people do some research for you when you are drawing up a proposal, writing a talk, etc.

5. Pace.

    a. Pace yourself. Use deadlines (for meetings, projects, mail, phone calls, etc.). (Are you familiar with Parkinson's Law which states that work expands to fit the time available?) By setting deadlines, you help yourself complete the job in a reasonable amount of time.

b. Work hard and don't be afraid to take breaks if you need them.

c. Reward yourself in some way for getting a hard job done.

d. Schedule tough jobs for when you are most likely to be in the right frame of mind and have the energy to do them.

e. Watch your eating habits. A huge lunch can really slow you down. As you work, you need your blood to be working for you in your head, not in your stomach. Did you ever hear about the professor who, after a big lunch, dreamed that he was teaching a class and then woke up to find out that he was?

6. Appointments.

a. Schedule an ending time as well as a beginning time for an appointment. One good way to do this is to schedule one appointment right after another. Your appointment will go more efficiently with a firm deadline.

b. Avoid scheduling 20-30 minutes between appointments. It is difficult to start something major in that period of time.

c. Always have something with you to do in case someone is late or for other reasons you have a few minutes free (e.g., write postcards, dictate letters, etc.).

d. During your appointment, give the person with you your undivided attention. Take as few phone calls as possible! Someone who has taken the trouble to come to your office and meet with you should take priority over the vast majority of phone calls. This way you will handle your business with him more quickly and will help him make the best use of his time.

e. Have your secretary step in or buzz you at the scheduled end of a meeting. This will accelerate your bringing it to a close.

7. Meetings.
    a. Five minutes of preparation for the meeting may save one hour in the meeting.
    b. Determine the objectives of the meeting: make decisions or recommendations, inform people, impart vision, have fellowship, etc.
    c. In counseling meetings, see if you can get to the issues as soon as possible. Talking is therapeutic to your counselee only to a point. You want to make sure you will have time during your session to apply God's Word to the problem.
    d. Schedule enough time for the meeting to accomplish its objectives but no more. Charles E. Wilson, who was a key mobilizer of American industry during World War II, was famous for his five-to-ten-minute meetings.
    e. Start on time.
    f. Work toward the objectives! Be leary of the statement, "Since we are here, we probably ought to discuss . . . "
    g. Consider holding conferences standing up or by phone if you want to accelerate them.
    h. Squeeze in meetings when you can, e.g., between appointments, during a meal, etc.

8. Communication tools.
    a. Once you read a piece of mail, do what is needed in response or file it or throw it away.
    b. Your secretary could be a great help in handling your mail by sorting it, answering much of it, etc. Even with the letters you personally see, she can take dictation from you or possibly write the letter for you after hearing a few key thoughts from you.
    c. Consider doing some of your personal correspondence by sending a cassette instead of sending a long letter. You can put more on tape in five to ten minutes than you can write in an hour.
    d. Use a phone call when it would take several letters

back and forth to communicate the same thing. This makes dollars and sense.

  e. When you don't want to be interrupted by phone calls, have someone take messages for you (or use an automatic telephone answering machine). Be sure to schedule time to answer messages at least every half day.

9. Reading.

  a. Look over a book before reading it. Determine what you want to get out of it.

  b. Read the book as rapidly as possible while still getting what you want out of the book.

  c. Take notes as you go and review them at the end.

  d. Have someone else read a book for you and review it with you if that is appropriate. Perhaps you can band together with a number of other people of similar interests and have each person in the group read a book of common interest and report on it to the group.

Conclusion

In summary, pray and think about what you do and how you do it. Aggressively seek ways to cause your activities to contribute more to what you are trying to accomplish. Be observant of what other people do to be more effective. Don't hesitate to discard the traditional in favor of the more functional. In the words of I Thessalonians 5:21, " . . . examine everything carefully; hold fast to that which is good."

As you do these things, you will multiply your time!

Before leaving this chapter, think back over what you have learned. Select one idea that seems as though it will be particularly helpful to you. Try to use this idea in the next few days.

7

Putting It All Together and Keeping at It

At this point, you have been exposed to quite a number of concepts, and I sincerely hope that you have gleaned many ideas that can be of use as you seek to manage yourself for the glory of God. In this concluding chapter of Part I, I would like to review quickly the various topics that have been covered so far, and give you another opportunity to apply some of the concepts if you have not done so already. Then I would like to share a few final thoughts that should help you get started on and keep at the ideas you have gleaned.

Review

The first topic covered involved the spiritual prerequisites to managing yourself. Chapter 2 presented material on how to know you are a Christian, how to deal with sin and how to walk with God. Do you feel you are walking closely with God, confessing sins to Him as they occur? Do you sense God's wisdom and power in your thoughts and actions?

If not, why not pause here and ask God to really be in control of your daily life? Walking closely with God is the best way I know of to help you manage yourself well.

The second topic involved planning long range. Chapter 3 presented a scriptural justification for planning, how to plan and opportunities for you to plan. You were given the opportunity to write down objectives for your life and to determine a specific objective for you to emphasize over the next six to twelve months. In addition, you were given the opportunity to determine the best way to accomplish that objective and to put the key elements of your planning on a 3x5 card to be placed in some often-viewed location. These things help you have overall purpose in what you do day by day. If you haven't finished your planning, set aside some time soon to do so.

The third topic involved scheduling your time. Chapter 4 presented a scriptural basis for scheduling, how to schedule, and opportunities for you to schedule. You learned the importance of first allowing time for your high priority activities. If you haven't yet planned a schedule for tomorrow, see if you can set aside a few minutes to do so before you go to bed tonight. It will help you be more productive and satisfied tomorrow.

The fourth topic involved following your schedule. Chapter 5 presented a scriptural basis for each principle. You learned about motivation, discipline, sensitivity and peace and how to claim each of them from God by faith. You were shown an example of how these principles fit into a person's daily life.

The fifth topic involved multiplying your time. Chapter 6 presented the scriptural importance of doing everything that we do in the best way. You learned of a general approach to improving the effectiveness of what you do. You also were given many specific ideas on how to save time and do things better.

These five topics cover the essentials of managing yourself. If you will seek to implement even some of these concepts in your life, you will become a more effective person.

How to Keep from Stopping

You have probably noticed by now that I have encouraged you to start implementing right away after you have learned a particular concept. My reason is that for most people the probability of ever implementing a newly learned concept goes down drastically as time passes. The old adage, "Do it now!" has a lot of wisdom in it.

Even if you have taken the first step of implementation, however, you are not out of the woods in terms of making the new concept a habit. Perhaps you have started on one of the ideas presented and you have discovered it is putting a strain on your schedule. Or perhaps something inside of you is resisting change. If so, review in your mind the benefits of what you are seeking to do. Why did you choose to read this book? Would it concern you if you were to not implement the improvement you are seeking? Don't the costs seem worth it in light of the benefits?

Pray and ask God to renew your motivation and supply the discipline that is needed to follow through. Growth as a person is not necessarily easy, but it is worth it, and it is something God is anxious to give us the power to do. Learning how to push through those times of low motivation is one of the most valuable lessons we can learn.

Whenever I share my faith in Christ, for example, there is always a moment when I seriously consider not doing it; I can come up with all kinds of reasons why the timing is inconvenient for me, or for the other person, or whatever. Knowing, however, that God would be pleased if I did share my faith, I find that the best thing to do is to ask Him for a special measure of discipline and simply to start sharing as an act of obedience.

As a further example, there were times while working on this book when I really didn't feel like dictating that next paragraph or outlining that next chapter. I thought of all sorts of reasons why these jobs should be put off until later, although I really knew that God wanted me to do them while I had the time. Again, the best solution was to pray for that special measure of discipline and simply to begin the job at hand. Once I got started, it became much easier to keep going.

Pace Yourself for the Long Haul

Sometimes we are tempted to quit because we start with such a flurry of enthusiasm and energy that we quickly "burn ourselves out." Among other things, I run for exercise. I have observed that on any given day there is a maximum speed at which I feel comfortable running. If I stay at that speed or under I can run for several miles. If I exceed that speed by very much, it may be all I can do to finish one mile. Therefore, if I intend to run a longer distance, I need to pace myself.

Life is a long-distance run, not a sprint, so it is very important that you set a pace for yourself that you can maintain for a long time. If you start off on something new with too much of a flurry, you may well perish at the end of the first mile and revert to the old way of doing things.

To avoid this situation, I would suggest that you concentrate for a while on just one main area of change at a time. Begin by choosing an area and keep that in your prayers and plans until it becomes a habit. Then you can focus on another area until it becomes a habit, and so on. If you find after a while that you can work on several areas of change at once, then by all means, do so. This will be easier to do as you become more comfortable with the managing yourself process, and as some of the results of your initial efforts serve to motivate you further.

Regarding the pace of your life in general, if you find yourself so busy that you are constantly fatigued, you now have some concepts to help you cut back on what is less important to you so that you can increase the emphasis on your true priorities.

On the other hand, if you feel that you are not accomplishing as much as you should overall, you will want to pick up the pace. You may want to begin to make more productive use of your evenings and weekends if you have been spending these almost exclusively in front of the TV. At any rate, whether you need to accelerate your pace or slow it down, be sure that the new pace is one that you can live with over the long haul.

You were created by God as a unique individual with interests, talents and circumstances all your own. Therefore, I would highly recommend that you adapt what you have been learning to your own situation in a way that maximizes your personal strengths and compensates for your weaknesses.

Harness Your Strengths

The question to ask yourself as you seek to maximize your strengths is, "What is it that I naturally enjoy doing and am already good at?" for that is what you will want to build on.

Let me give you an example of building on a strength. I find that I am most alert for the first several hours after I have been sleeping, even if I have only had a nap. I built on this personal characteristic of mine while writing this book. The first significant amount of time I spent on it was during a week-long vacation with my wife in the mountains near San Bernardino. When I began to run out of gas in my efforts, I would put down my pencil and dictating equipment and go take an hour's nap. I would then wake up refreshed to work for another several hours. It would have been unproductive to have tried to push on at a very uncreative level while I was drowsy, when one hour later I could be at my peak alertness.

By the same token, I am a "morning person," and I build on this trait by having my time of personal Bible study before the day begins, which is no problem for me. I know others who can study well late at night, but it would be unrealistic for me to think that, if I miss my early morning study, I can make it up very meaningfully at the end of the day.

The key is to know yourself and not to fight what you can harness. Learn what it is that you do most naturally and then build on those strengths so that you can accomplish the things God really wants you to do in life.

Compensate for Your Weaknesses

Just as you can harness your strengths and maximize them, so can you compensate for your weaknesses as you seek to improve in these areas.

It may be that as a result of reading this book you have become aware of a weakness in your life. Fortunately, you can benefit immediately from that awareness even though it may take some time to see significant change in that area of your life. For once you know something is a weakness, you can compensate for it through the help of other people for whom the area is a strength.

A most obvious source of help would be your spouse. If he or she happens to have a strength in your area of weakness, perhaps you could work out an arrangement in which your spouse would take on the activity that you don't do well, and you could offer to help your spouse in some other area.

For example, my wife, Judy, and I both work full time, and yet often have guests over for dinner. With all that needs to be done in preparation for our guests, we both need to pitch in to make it possible. Judy really loves to cook and is good at it. I, on the other hand, don't especially enjoy cooking and am not good at it. Judy doesn't enjoy picking up and vacuuming, but I do. Our vacuum cleaner is fairly heavy and hard to handle for Judy, whereas I enjoy vacuuming as a little exercise. Therefore, Judy cooks, and I pick up things and vacuum. This way we each do what we enjoy and avoid what would be more difficult.

Another obvious area in which you can compensate for your weakness is your job. For example, if you are somewhat weak at thinking of new ideas, you would probably be wise to include a creative thinker in your planning sessions.

On the other hand, if your weakness is in following through, you would want to ask someone who is skilled in this area to help you with control and project management.

Be sensitive to opportunities to compensate for your weaknesses while you are learning to strengthen them.

Share Your Learning with Others

As a final help in making the best use of what you have learned about managing yourself, I recommend that you seek to pass along that learning to someone else. For even if you just share the one concept that has been most meaningful to you with one other person, I think you will find the experience very helpful in consolidating your knowledge of the subject matter. And, of course, you may very well stimulate someone else to positive action.

I recognize from my own experience that the things I know the best are the things that I teach. I teach a Sunday school class, for example, and I have to really know the Bible passages before I can pass them on to my students. The result is that I learn more than if I were studying the passage for my own benefit alone.

Conclusion

This concludes Part I of the book. What you have read is a course in the basics of managing yourself. If you are faithful to apply these concepts, you will greatly improve your personal effectiveness.

Part II, which follows, presents more in-depth concepts on knowing God's will, planning long range and scheduling your time. It also includes several chapters to stimulate your thinking on how to improve in the various general areas of your life: spiritual, mental, physical, social, vocational, financial and family.

PART II
Beyond the Basics:
Tools For Further Effectiveness

The following chapters provide more in-depth material on managing yourself. The concepts presented supplement what you learned in Part I. Part I provides a framework for operating in life which is very adequate for most people. Part II helps you refine and enhance your personal effectiveness even further.

Before carefully reading and implementing the suggested application in a chapter in Part II, I suggest you skim through it first. This skimming may well give you what you would seek from that chapter at this time and will give you the ability to reference the chapter later when you feel a more significant need in that subject area. If, however, you sense you could greatly benefit from the content of the chapter now, dig in and read it thoroughly.

8

More on Planning Long Range

The purpose of this chapter is to give you a more in-depth exposure to planning long range. You were given enough material to get you started planning in Chapter 3 in Part I. You were encouraged to jot down your initial thinking on your life objectives. In this chapter you will have the opportunity to refine your thoughts in light of some additional concepts.

In Chapter 3 you came up with your number one priority objective for the next six to twelve months and the number one priority activity to accomplish that objective. In this chapter you will have the opportunity to broaden your planning to include more priorities and to be more comprehensive in your thinking on them.

Benefits of Planning

Planning yields some very tangible benefits to you. The first is that you will normally spend less total time on a project if you plan it well. If you don't think out something before you start, very often you have to backtrack or you observe a better way after you are too far along to change. As a result, you take an unwarranted amount of time doing the project. If, on the other hand, you take the time needed to plan, you normally much more than save that time doing the project faster.

Second, planning greatly reduces fire-fighting. A good portion of many people's days is spent trying to solve one "crisis" after another. Problems seem to spring forth from every corner and we often feel like a ping-pong ball being bounced back and forth. Those are the days in which we usually say, "I didn't get anything done today!"

Planning helps cure this kind of situation in two ways. Often we can anticipate certain problems and either prevent them or at least provide for them in advance, thus reducing the disabling "crisis" mentality. Also, when we are stretching to achieve a worthwhile objective, many things that seemed of "crisis" proportion before don't really seem that significant a priority anymore; thus we don't bother with them.

Explanation of How to Plan

In Chapter 3 you were briefly exposed to a five-step outline on how to plan: pray, establish objectives, program, schedule and budget. The following is a further explanation of each of these steps.

Step No. One: Pray

In this step you make sure that you are appropriating God's wisdom for your plan. For if the plan is not what God intends, you will just be wasting your own time and the time of those around you as the plan is implemented.

You may find it helpful, as I do, to go about appropriating God's wisdom in the following way.

First, thank God that you have the wisdom of the mind of Christ. "For who has known the mind of the Lord, that he should instruct Him? But **we have** the mind of Christ" (I Corinthians 2:16).

Next, ask God for specific wisdom. "But if any of you lacks wisdom, let him ask of God, who gives to all men generously and without reproach, and it will be given to him" (James 1:5).

Then, commit to Him what you are about to plan. "Commit your works to the Lord, and your plans will be established" (Proverbs 16:3).

Finally, write down any thoughts or Scriptures that God impresses upon your mind concerning your plan. Sometimes God will lead you to a very unconventional approach. Imagine Joshua's thoughts when the Lord outlined the plan for taking Jericho (Joshua 6:2-5)!

Step No. 2: Establish Objectives

In this step you determine **what** it is that should be accomplished. You set a goal or target toward which you and the people with whom you work will be directing your efforts. To many people, planning is merely filling in a budget form or a yearly calendar. And yet how can you possibly determine how much money will be spent or when different activities need to take place until you have determined what it is that should be accomplished?

Your objectives are criteria against which you can measure the appropriateness of all your current activities.

It demonstrates your trust in God to prayerfully ask Him for His objectives and not just what you could do in your own strength without Him.

Step No. 3: Program

After determining what should be accomplished, it seems logical that the next step should be to determine **how** to accomplish your objectives. You need to decide on the steps or activities that will best get you from where you are now to your desired outcome. These steps may be in sequence, that is to say, one step logically follows the other until the goal is reached, or they may be activities that occur simultaneously.

Step No. 4: Schedule

This is the step that makes your plan workable on a day-to-day basis. Here you determine **when** the different steps of your program should take place. You take those steps or activities and place them in actual time slots on a calendar or schedule so that you will know exactly when each one should begin and end. You also enter on the schedule target numbers or milestones to help you determine progress toward your objectives.

Step No. 5: Budget

Many practical issues are faced in this step. You determine **how much** will be needed in the way of money, manpower, materials, etc., in order to implement your plan. Then you determine just **how** these needs will be **supplied**. Don't forget that, if God called you to the objective at the beginning of the plan, He is not going to deny you the resources required to see it through: "And my God shall supply all your needs according to His riches in glory in Christ Jesus" (Philippians 4:19).

Applying This to Your Life

Now I would like to give you the opportunity to plan for your life. I will mention when your previous planning from Chapter 3 may save you a step. Otherwise, what follows will be additionally beneficial to you.

First, take time to pray. We have seen that the initial step in effective planning is to ask God for His wisdom in our lives. This is only reasonable because God alone knows what lies ahead, and He alone truly understands our various capabilities. He also knows how we will react under conditions of stress and in light of specific things that will happen to us in the future.

Therefore, to launch you in the planning process, I would like to ask you now to take some time and ask God specifically what He wants for your life. You will be seeking direction here concerning objectives for your life as a whole. When you blow out the candles on your 80th birthday cake, what is it that you hope will have been accomplished during all those years?

As mentioned earlier, you can claim God's promise to give you wisdom without reproach (James 1:5). You can also claim His promise to actually establish plans in your mind as you commit your future to Him (Proverbs 16:3). And you can **know** that you have the very mind of Christ (I Corinthians 2:16). Pause here and pray.

Write Down Basic Thoughts

Now that you have taken time to ask God for His wisdom concerning your life objectives, I would like to ask you to take a clean sheet of paper and jot down the kinds of things that came to mind as you prayed. Just take a few minutes here to record your basic thoughts. We will be refining these as we go through the chapter, so what is most important now is that you capture the essence of anything that God may have shown you just now, or, for that matter, that He may have been showing you for some time. If the life objectives you wrote down in Chapter 3 serve this purpose, go on to the next paragraph. Otherwise, pause here and write down your thoughts.

What Does the Bible Say?

Now put aside your sheet for a moment and let's take a look at what the Bible has to say about some of the objectives that should be common to all of us as Christians. I would like to direct your attention specifically to three passages of Scripture:

Sing to the Lord a new song; Sing to the Lord, all the earth. Sing to the Lord, bless His name; Proclaim good tidings of His salvation from day to day. Tell of His glory among the nations, His wonderful deeds among all the peoples. For great is the Lord, and greatly to be praised; He is to be feared above all gods. For all the gods of the peoples are idols, But the Lord made the heavens. Splendor and majesty are before Him, Strength and beauty are in His sanctuary (Psalms 96:1-6).

I glorified Thee on the earth, having accomplished the work which Thou hast given Me to do (John 17:4).

And the four living creatures, each one of them having six wings, are full of eyes around and within; and day and night they do not cease to say, "Holy, Holy, Holy, is the Lord God, the Almighty, who was and who is and who is to come." And when the living creatures give glory and honor and thanks to Him who sits on the throne, to Him who lives forever and ever, the twenty-four elders will fall down before Him who sits on the throne, and will worship Him who lives forever and ever, and will cast their crowns before the throne, saying, "Worthy art Thou, our Lord and our God, to receive glory and honor and power; for Thou didst create all things, and because of Thy will they existed, and were created" (Revelation 4:8-11).

What theme do you see among these three passages? In the first one, the psalmist enthusiastically exhorts us to glorify and praise God and to tell others about His glory on a daily basis. In the second passage, Jesus Christ, in a conversation with the Father, speaks of having glorified the Father through His life on earth. In the third passage, we get an indication of what heaven is like, and it appears that a major activity there is the glorifying of God.

Glorify God

The one common overall objective for us as Christians, in my judgment, is that we **glorify God**.

If our basic objective in life is to glorify God, an activity in which we engage ought to be in some way glorifying to Him. Therefore, a good way to determine whether or not our various activities are even basically appropriate is to ask the simple question, "Is this glorifying to God?" The answer is usually fairly obvious.

For the purposes of being more specific, though, let us look again to the Scriptures to get some details on just what is involved in glorifying God. I would again like to direct your attention to three specific passages.

Be a Disciple

For whom He foreknew, He also predestined to become conformed to the image of His Son, that He might be the first-born among many brethren (Romans 8:29).

Here we see the intention of God to conform us to the image of Jesus Christ. God wants us to become increasingly like Him as we grow and mature as Christians. We should increasingly know and implement the Scriptures in our lives as disciples. This is the objective that probably ranks above all others toward contributing to our overall objective of glorifying God.

Disciple Other Christians

Go therefore and make disciples of all the nations, baptizing them in the name of the Father and the Son and the Holy Spirit, teaching them to observe all that I commanded you; and lo, I am with you always, even to the end of the age (Matthew 28:19,20).

Here we see God's intention that we minister to other Christians, building them up in the faith, or discipling them. This is another objective that would greatly contribute to our overall objective of glorifying God.

Share the Gospel with Non-Christians

> But you shall receive power when the Holy Spirit has
> come upon you; and you shall be My witnesses both in
> Jerusalem, and in all Judea and Samaria, and even to
> the remotest part of the earth (Acts 1:8).

Here we see God's intention that we proclaim the gospel
to all those who have not heard it. This, then, constitutes a
third objective that would greatly contribute to our overall
objective.

John 15:8 summarizes these ways of glorifying God: "By
this is My Father glorified, that you bear much fruit, and so
prove to be My disciples."

Being a disciple, discipling other Christians, and sharing
the gospel with non-Christians can be found throughout the
Scriptures as objectives for Christians. The following are a
few additional passages of Scripture for your further study:
Luke 19:10; Matthew 9:35-38; Galatians 5:22,23; II Peter
3:9-15; II Timothy 2:2. Activities which contribute toward
these objectives should be high priority for the Christian.

As you consider these three more specific objectives, you
might be somewhat staggered by the magnitude of what they
could involve in your life. Just remember that these are objectives to pursue over a lifetime, and none of us ever fully
achieves on earth all that is implied by these verses. The important thing is that we make progress toward these at the
pace that God sets for us.

At this point, I would like to ask you to go back to your
sheet of paper and take a few minutes to add to or refine
your initial thoughts in light of what the Scriptures have to
say about the overall objective of glorifying God and the
related lifetime objectives of being a disciple, discipling other
Christians, and sharing the gospel with non-Christians. Pause
here and write down your thoughts.

No Carbon Copies

Just as it is true that there are objectives we should all be pursuing as Christians, so are there personal objectives that God would have for each of us as individuals. In God's kingdom there are no carbon copies—each of us is unique with different talents, interests and capabilities, and God has a special plan for each of our lives.

Psalms 139:16 tells us that even before we were born, God ordained our days. I Peter 4:10 further reveals that each of us has received a special gift from God to be used according to His purpose. And in Ephesians 4:16 we are told that, in order for the body of Christ (sum total of all believers) to grow and function properly, each individual member must be doing his part.

I happen to have a mild case of "tennis elbow," and whenever I want to put a little extra spin on my tennis serve, I find myself holding back because I know that my elbow will hurt. Using this analogy, if I am supposed to be an elbow, let's say, in Christ's body, and I have "tennis elbow" and don't function properly, I could be the reason for other Christians around me not functioning in the best possible way.

If there are very many members of Christ's body who are not doing their part, local groups of believers will lurch and lunge like Frankenstein's monster as they attempt to fulfill their objectives here on earth! So it is important for each of us to know as much as God will reveal to us of His objectives for us as individuals.

God's Will for Your Life

At this point, I am going to ask you to return once again to your sheet of paper in order to further refine your objectives in light of these new thoughts. If you already have a pretty strong idea of what it is that God has especially for you to do in life, then by all means write that down if you haven't already.

If, however, you are not sure what God has specifically called you to do, I would suggest you read Chapter 9, "Knowing God's Will for Your Life." That material is designed to help you gain a clearer understanding of God's design for you as an individual. It is important that you have some knowledge of this, because it is difficult to prioritize your activities without knowing what you are trying to accomplish.

Often, God only reveals to us a portion of His plan at a time. Whatever God chooses to reveal will be adequate for us to know how we should be spending our time month to month and day to day. Now, read through Chapter 9 if necessary, and/or pause here to further refine your life objectives.

Let's Consider Short-term Objectives

At this point in our planning, we are going to move from general lifetime objectives to a consideration of specific objectives for the next six to twelve months. The advantage of shorter-term objectives is that normally you can begin to shoot for them right away. Although you could conceivably think through a program, schedule and budget for your entire life, I have found that for most people, detailed planning for a whole lifetime is too elaborate a task. So instead, let's just focus on what you would like to see accomplished in the next six to twelve months.

Take out a fresh sheet of paper and write down specific objectives you would like to see come true in your life in the next six to twelve months. These should be specific and conceivably achievable in the next six to twelve months. They may be actual achievements or they may be improvements you would like to see in your life, e.g., in the area of personal Bible study. Just take a minute or two to capture the most obvious ideas. After this, I will help you add a few items to your list. Pause here and write down the things that seem most important to you. Include the number one objective you determined in Chapter 3 at the top of this list.

Influenced by Life Objectives?

Were you influenced by your life objectives as you were writing? If not, read back through these and ask if there is something you could do in the next six to twelve months to move in the direction of your life objectives.

What Phase Are You In?

Next I would like for you to think with me about what phase of life you find yourself in. With regard to career, most people's lives follow this pattern:
1. A time of growing up and receiving initial education and training.
2. A time in which work is begun and initial experience is gained in the work area and in other facets of life.
3. A main productive period for work and other pursuits.
4. A more thoughtful and less energetic time in which we have a maximum of experience, but our bodies are not quite as strong and able as they used to be.

With regard to marriage and family, the following are the typical phases:
1. Single.
2. Married with no children.
3. Married with pre-school children.
4. Married with school-age children who are home in the evening.
5. Married with grown children who do not live at home.

Of course, your own situation will be a combination of these phases depending on the number and ages of your children and depending on your progress in your career. In whichever phases you find yourself at present, though, there are probably some specific objectives you should be considering relative to those phases.

For example, an objective for parents with pre-school children would be the discipling of those children while they are still in their most formative years. By the time a child goes to school, his relationship with God should be developed as far as he is willing and able to comprehend, because from then on he will likely face increasingly corrosive influences to that relationship.

Another example would involve people who are newly married and have not yet started a family. One obvious decision would be if and when to try to have children. Once a family is underway, there will naturally be many other objectives to consider.

As another example, the young person just getting out of high school or college faces the decision of where to go to work. It may be possible just to start with one firm and stay with it for a major portion of one's life. However, before beginning job-hunting, it would certainly be a good idea to consider what kind of initial work experiences would be appropirate for the long-term career objective.

As a final example, people facing what we call "retirement" might do well to think through the kinds of objectives God would have for them during this period of life. I personally feel it would be a great mistake to assume that we should just play golf and sip tea for the rest of our lives. Retirement is a phase that offers wonderful opportunities to minister to others because time is available, finances are provided for, and experience is at a maximum.

Consider the Areas of Your Life

As a last stimulus to your thinking, let me propose to you seven areas or categories of your life in which you may want to have short-term objectives: spiritual, mental, physical, social, vocational, financial and family.

Are there specific improvements you would like in these areas of your life? For example, in the spiritual area: How is your prayer life? Has God been impressing you with regard to some specific quality of life, e.g., love, holiness, etc.? Another example is the physical area: Are you at the right weight? Are you eating the right foods?

Chapters 11-17 of this book cover each of these areas of life in much more depth. The purpose of this exposure is simply to start stimulating your thinking.

Now, I would like to ask you to return to your initial list of short-term objectives and add to it in light of any new thoughts that may have occurred to you. Don't write down too many new thoughts so as to be overwhelmed; just write down the new ideas that seem to be particularly helpful to you now. Pause here and write down your thoughts.

Let's Assign Priorities

What I would like for you to do now is to assign priorities to your list of short-term objectives and determine which **one** of them you would **most** like to see accomplished over the next six to twelve months. If only one could be accomplished, which would be the best one? This will be your number one priority. It could contribute to the fulfillment of a specific, stated lifetime objective, or it could be something that simply needs to be accomplished in your life right now, like losing weight. Put a "1" to the left of that objective. In light of the new input, this may or may not be the same as your number one objective from Chapter 3.

When you have done that, select a number two objective. When your number one objective is removed from consideration, which of the remaining objectives would you most like to see accomplished? Put a "2" by that. Next, select a number three priority. Pause here and determine your priority objectives.

In about six to twelve months, you will probably want to add to your list and prioritize your objectives again. At this point, however, I would like for you to plan out your number one priority objective. To assist you in this, there is an example of a planning worksheet on the last page of this chapter.

As you can see, the person who did this planning followed the planning outline. As you proceed with your planning, I would suggest you use the same format for your planning worksheet. Start by writing out your number one priority objective for the next six to twelve months at the top of a fresh sheet of paper. Pause here and do that.

Before leaving the "establish objectives" point, I find it is helpful to jot down a few of the benefits of achieving the objective. Many times the reason an objective is number one is that it has been put off for some time. To help cure that problem, among others, it is good to have before you why you want to do what you are attempting. Note how the example includes the benefits. Pause here and add to your worksheet why you want to accomplish your number one objective.

Program

Now you are ready to program. That is to say, you are ready to determine how your objective can best be accomplished. What steps are needed to take you from where you are now to your desired outcome?

It may well be that a straightforward "step 1, step 2, step 3" will come to mind. If this is the case, then by all means simply write out and number those steps.

If you need help at this, I have personally found it useful to begin programming an objective by picturing in my mind what will actually be going on in my life when the objective is accomplished. Try calling to mind as vivid a picture as you can of your objective as an accomplished fact. Include all the details you can think of. For example, if your objective is to improve your personal Bible study, you should picture yourself as actually having a better study. You should visualize yourself doing such things as getting up earlier, getting something meaningful out of the Word, thinking about what you were learning, applying it, etc.

Now these things you visualized should stimulate in your mind particular program activities. For example, if you pictured yourself getting up earlier in the morning, you will have to take certain steps for this to occur, such as putting your alarm clock further from the bed to insure that you will get up, etc.

As you go through this process, you may begin to see the problems or barriers that have kept you from accomplishing your objective in the past. You see, for example, that you weren't able to have an effective early morning Bible study because you were getting to bed too late. One reason we fail to overcome barriers is that we fail to recognize them. Now, as you become aware of these barriers, the steps of your program can seek to overcome them.

Use Brainstorming If Necessary

Another technique that is helpful in programming is simply to think of as many different ways as possible to move in the direction of accomplishing the objective. This is the technique used in the example. The person tried to think of the various ways he could get in better shape. When you are brainstorming, write down every idea without evaluation. Evaluation comes later. While brainstorming you want to be creative, thinking new thoughts in addition to documenting old ones.

After brainstorming, you should look over the list to see if there is a natural sequence to some of the ideas. You will also notice that some of the ideas do not seem as productive as others. If you can select a logical first activity, place "1" in front of it. Place "2" in front of the next in sequence, etc. You will probably end up leaving out several of the ideas because they are not necessary.

If the ideas don't fall into a natural sequence, there is one last approach that will always work. Look over your list of ideas and select the one which seems most likely to take you the longest distance toward accomplishing your objective. Place "1" in front of that idea. This is what the person did in the example. He rejected running because he doesn't enjoy it. He rejected push-ups and sit-ups because they are not particularly "wind" exercises. He rejected walking because it would take too much time. He rejected the health club idea because he was short of money at the time.

Pause here and determine the best program to accomplish your number one objective. Use whatever technique seems to suit your situation best. If your planning from Chapter 3 helps you here, by all means use it.

Schedule and Budget

Although not always necessary, it is usually helpful to consider the implications of timing and resources even on a simple plan. At a minimum it is good to think through the details on getting started on your number one program activity. In the example the person determined that he needed to buy a jump rope from a nearby sporting goods or department store. He felt the price of the rope was easily within his means. He set a target for himself of spending 10 minutes a day in the morning. He saw no reason he couldn't buy one the next day and get started the following morning.

Pause here and apply this point in your planning.

Keep Your Plan Where You Can See It

It is very important that you keep your plan in some prominent place where you will see it often. One way to do that would be to attach your worksheet to the side of your closet or on a bulletin board at home. Another would be to write out the number one program activity on a 3x5 card and tape it to a mirror that you look into every morning.

Chapters 4 and 10 give more information on how to systematically seek to include your number one activity in your daily or weekly schedule. However, it is not possible to be overexposed to reminders for something that is important, since this is the one thing that contributes to what is most important to you in terms of accomplishment. You don't want to take any chances that it is going to be forgotten admidst the many other things you are doing.

Conclusion

Many times we are the victims of complexity, and I certainly do not intend for you to get bogged down here. If, however, you feel you would like to go a little further in your planning, proceed to program, schedule, and budget your number two and three objectives. In each case, write down the objective at the top of a fresh sheet of paper, determine the benefits, etc.

In conclusion, you have had the opportunity in this chapter to learn more about the planning process. You have been given the opportunity to do some detailed thinking about how to determine and pursue personal objectives. As you apply this, it should prove to be an effective instrument which God can use to communicate to you specific directions for your life.

EXAMPLE OF PERSONAL PLANNING

Objective:
>   Be in better shape physically. Achieve at least the mini-
>   mum suggested level in Dr. Cooper's book, *The New
>   Aerobics*.
>   Benefits: Feel better; fight heart and other diseases; be
>   able to climb the stairs at work without becoming
>   winded.

Program:
>   Run
> 1 Jump rope
>   Do push-ups and sit-ups
>   Walk
>   Join health club and exercise there

Schedule and Budget:
>   Buy rope tomorrow ($5 estimated cost).
>   Start following morning.
>   Jump and rest alternately for 10 minutes.

9

Knowing God's Will
for Your Life

Some of us have a pretty good idea of what God's will for our lives is; others of us are less sure about this. At any rate, all of us can benefit from help at some time or other in determining what God would have us do. Therefore, I would like to share with you nine concepts that have been of great value to me in this area. I hope that they will be of use to you as well.

Be Filled with the Spirit

The best way to know God's will in any situation is to be sure that you are filled with God's Spirit. (The specifics of this command from Ephesians 5:18 are dealt with in Chapter 2.) When you are walking in the Spirit—that is to say, when God is in control of your life—you will know what He would have you do, for He will put His thoughts in your mind, and you will find that you are doing the right thing.

Proverbs 3:5,6 confirms the fact that, if you "trust in the Lord with all your heart" and "in all your ways acknowledge Him," He will direct your path in life.

This step of being sure you are filled with God's Spirit is by far the most significant concept I can mention.

Pray for Wisdom

Remember the claim of James 1:5, "But if any of you lacks wisdom, let him ask of God who gives to all men generously and without reproach, and it will be given to him." God has promised to give us wisdom on any matter, and that would certainly include wisdom concerning His will for your life or concerning a specific situation you are facing.

Consider Scriptural Objectives

As mentioned in Chapters 3 and 8, the Scriptures outline three basic objectives that should be common to all of us as Christians. John 15:8 provides a good summary of those objectives: "But by this is My Father glorified, that you bear much fruit, and so prove to be My disciples." According to this verse, we are to bear much fruit (in the lives of non-believers as we witness to them, and in the lives of other Christians as we seek to disciple them), and we are to be disciples of Christ ourselves, becoming increasingly conformed to His image. Thus will we glorify God.

As you seek to determine God's will, you can know that these are objectives He would have for you. Therefore, it would be wise to focus on these as you make life-affecting decisons.

Take All Scripture into Account

In II Timothy 3:16,17, we learn that "all Scripture is inspired by God and profitable for teaching, for reproof, for correction, for training in righteousness; that the man of God may be adequate, equipped for every good work."

It would be most appropriate to test whatever it is you are thinking of doing against what the Scriptures have to say on the subject. Let the Scriptures serve as a boundary for your activities, keeping you within the territory of God's will. For example, if you are thinking of becoming a go-go dancer in the local bar, I think you would quickly perceive through an examination of the Scriptures that this is not an activity that God would have you consider.

Also take into account any Scriptures that God has impressed on your mind over a period of time when such Scriptures relate to the decision you are trying to make.

Consider Facts about Yourself   _consider past_

Carefully examine your strengths: the gifts God has given you, the talents that you have, your education, your past experience and so forth. Psalms 37:23 tells us that "the steps of a man are established by the Lord." You can be certain that God has not placed in your life anything that will not be useful to you in some way, as you seek to do His will.

When I joined the staff of Campus Crusade for Christ, I asked for a job in the area of business administration. My decision to ask to work in this area was based on a careful examination of what I felt God had given me. For example, God had given me a master's degree in the subject, and good stewardship seemed to indicate that I use it. In addition, my interest was in that area as was my past experience.

Manford Gutzke, an outstanding Bible teacher from Columbia Bible College, really dwells on this idea of looking to your past to help determine God's will for your life. Particularly if you have allowed God to direct your life for some time, you will find in your past many indicators of what it is that you should be doing in the future. Don't abandon all that past leading. Don't think that, when you get out of bed tomorrow, God is going to suddenly contradict what He has carefully shown you in the past. I don't have to ask God every day, for example, if I should stay on the staff of Campus Crusade for Christ. God has already given me leading in that regard and I needn't question it unless He were specifically to reveal to me otherwise.

Consider Counsel

Proverbs 11:14 tells us, "In abundance of counselors there is victory." In many cases, it would be appropriate for you to seek the advice of godly men and women whose judgment you respect. Although you will probably receive more specific ideas than you can implement, the pattern or focus of the counsel can be an excellent indicator of God's will.

Consider Impressions

Philippians 2:13 tells us that "it is God who is at work within you, both to will and to work for His good pleasure." In John 10:27 Christ says, "My sheep hear My voice, . . . and they follow Me." Both of these verses seem to indicate that God speaks to us through impressions.

If God is in control of our lives and our "spiritual antennae" are up, we are able to receive the impressions God has for us. Of course, impressions can be deceptive in that they can also come from sources other than God. However, if you are walking in the Spirit, and a certain impression that is consistent with the Scriptures keeps coming back to you, day after day and week after week, and you have asked God to cause you to forget the impression if it is not from Him, and this has not occurred, then I think you can normally assume that the impression is from the Lord.

Perhaps the most striking example of an impression from the Lord in my own life occurred when I was given the responsibility to find within three months a director for a particular Campus Crusade for Christ ministry in Florida. I appointed a temporary director for three months and then began my search. The three months went by with no director in sight. My only course of action at that point was to assume the full directorship of the ministry myself. I did this rather reluctantly, I might add, since I still had my regular responsibilities at Campus Crusade's headquarters in San Bernardino, California, and I did not relish holding two full-time jobs several thousand miles apart!

A couple of days later, while having devotions in my Florida office early Monday morning, I came across the passage in John 15 that says, "If you abide in Me and My words abide in you, ask whatever you wish, and it shall be done for you." No sooner had I read these words than I "heard" a voice within me saying, almost audibly, "Do you believe that verse?"

"Ask that you have your director by Friday," the impression continued.

"Now wait a minute," I replied. "I've been trying for 90 days to find that director, and there isn't a warm lead left that I know of. I can't possibly have a director by Friday."

"Do you believe that verse?" was the recurring thought in my mind.

"Yes," I replied. "All Scripture is inspired by You, Lord."

"Then pray that you have your director by Friday."

Somewhat hesitatingly, I prayed that a director would be known to me and would be available by Friday, and then I finished my devotions.

By that time it was about 8 a.m., and off to the side of my desk were a number of messages. As I reached for them, my fingers seemed to gravitate toward one in particular. It simply said, "Call Warren Brock," and gave a phone number in Fort Lauderdale. Now I didn't know anyone by the name of Warren Brock; for all I knew, he could have been our banker. At any rate, I called him up.

The first thing he said to me after a preliminary exchange of greetings was, "I understand you are looking for a director." He went on to say that his background was in insurance, which was just the background that was needed, and that he had recently quit his job for various reasons and was available if we would consider him. A couple of days later, he was approved for the job.

I have wondered several times just what the Lord would have done with that phone message if I had not been willing to trust Him and had not prayed as I had been instructed. Do you suppose it would have simply self-destructed like the recorded assignments on "Mission Impossible"? I'm not sure. But one thing I do know is that, though He doesn't always work this way, God can convey His will to us by way of impressions.

Weigh the Pros and Cons

I Corinthians 2:15 tells us that "he who is spiritual appraises all things," and in verse 16 we are told that, as Christians, we have the mind of Christ. Weighing the pros and cons of the various alternatives is a way that we can use the sound mind that God has given us.

One way to do this is to list your alternatives across the top of a clean sheet of paper. Under each alternative you can make a column in which you list the pros, or plus points, and the cons, or minus points of each alternative. Then you can look over what you've written and more readily determine which of the alternatives makes the most sense.

Ask for God's Confirming Peace

In Colossians 3:15 we are told to "let the peace of Christ rule in your hearts." Ask God to give you a peace about a decision you have tentatively made as further confirmation that it is His will for you. Waiting for this is especially important when making significant decisions.

Before I made the decision to propose to Judy, who is now my wife, I dated her for quite some time. After a while, it seemed possible that God would have us marry one another. For some reason, however, God did not give me a peace about it. Perhaps this lack of peace related to the travel then involved in my job and the things the Lord had for me to do. Perhaps it related to the fact that I was not ready to be constrained by marriage. Or perhaps it related to some of the things that God was doing in Judy's life of which I was unaware. Whatever the reason, God would not give me a sense of peace deep down within my heart that this was the right step, and I was not about to move ahead without that peace. Marriage is an irrevocable decision, and I needed to be absolutely certain that this was what God intended.

When God finally did give me the confirming peace I was looking for, I proposed to Judy.

Conclusion

The above nine concepts can help you as you seek God's will for you life. They can also help as you make other decisions and want God's specific wisdom.

Remember that the surest and most significant way you can know God's will is to be sure that you are filled with His Spirit and are indeed walking in that Spirit, allowing God to control and empower your life. As you walk closely with God, He will normally use some or all of the other eight concepts to define the specifics of the revelation of His will to you. Also, though, you can be assured that, as you walk with Him, you are in His will, regardless of how much you have yet specifically come to know about it.

10

Scheduling Your Week

In Chapter 4 you learned how to schedule for a small block of time and for a day. Now I would like to show you how the same scheduling outline applies to a week. The busier you are and the more diverse and complex your activities are, the more you will benefit from scheduling further ahead than one day at a time.

As you may recall, the scheduling of any block of time involves four basic steps: list activities, ask if assignable, assess priorities and schedule. The following is how these steps apply to the scheduling of a week.

Step No. 1: List Activities

Pray for wisdom and then list your potential activities for the next week. The following is a checklist of sources of potential activities:
1. Time with God and with your family.
2. Time for personal well-being (adequate sleep, meals, relaxation, physical exercise, etc.).
3. Time to plan for the following week.

4. Major activities from your long-range planning. This includes plans for your work and for your personal and family life. Be sure to include your number one priority activity toward your number one objective.
5. Appointments, social commitments, etc., from your personal calendar.
6. Any regular commitments you might have (e.g., a meeting every Monday, 10-12 a.m., etc.).
7. Major work assignments (projects, correspondence, phone calls, visits, etc.).
8. Activities from other calendars (secretary's, wife's, etc.).
9. Other things that have come up (recent assignments, items from other weeks that did not get done, etc.).

Step No. 2: Ask If Assignable

Next, go over each of the activities on your list and determine if any of them can be assigned to someone else.

Remember that many of the things you do could be done by others. For example, you may be able to ask your secretary to answer much of your business mail, composing letters from outlines from you. Look carefully at each activity to distinguish between things you should do and things you should assign.

Be on guard for the pendulum effect as you assign activities. If you haven't assigned much before, you may think it works like magic at first. You tell someone else to do an activity and then cross it off your list. A little later you discover it isn't done so you take it back. There is more to assigning than just telling someone. When you do make an assignment, be sure that you give adequate instruction to the person who is to be responsible. Be available for questions. Decide when you should follow up on an assigned activity and make a note of this on your calendar. At the appropriate time take the initiative to ask the person about the activity. Be available to help, but do so only if help is needed and wanted.

Step No. 3: Assess Priorities

The next step is to assess the priorities of the remaining activities. As you go about this procedure, think about 1) how **important** each activity is in accomplishing your objectives, and 2) how **urgent** it is that you do the activity this week. See Chapter 4 for a more complete explanation of the integration of importance and urgency into one overall priority rating. Do not constantly sacrifice the important items for those that are urgent. Don't immediately assume an activity is important just because you do it often.

As you assign priorities, you could use the numerical system that we used in scheduling in Chapter 4; however, the following ranking system would probably be more suited to your purposes here:
T = top priority
H = high priority
M = medium priority
L = low priority
With a longer list of potential activities, it should be easier to approximate if an activity is top, high, medium or low priority than if it is priority 16, 17, 18 or whatever.

Very few priorities deserve top ranking. These would include time with God, time with your family and time for personal well-being, though you may have others as well. Many activities deserve a high ranking. Many others rate a medium. And there are many activities that should be given a low ranking.

Step No. 4: Schedule

The final step is to actually place your activities onto a weekly schedule in the order of their priority. (It is a good idea to use a pencil instead of a pen in this step so that you can make corrections and changes as needed.)

First of all, place on your schedule any already-committed-to appointments which are top or high priority, such as scheduled meetings at which your presence is required. Next, enter medium or low priority appointments, placing dotted lines around the time slots for these. The purpose of placing firm commitments on your schedule right away is so that you will not schedule other activities during the time these commitments are due to take place. The use of dotted lines around medium and low priority appointments highlights the fact that you may want to displace these later with higher priority activities.

Now it may be that over a period of time you will find that some activities occur regularly every week, are always top or high priority and always go on your schedule in the same time slot. If that is the case, your time scheduling procedures can be streamlined by simply entering such activities onto your schedule directly instead of first listing them, asking if they are assignable and assessing their priority. You should still review the priority and assignability of such activities every few months, however.

Once your committed-to appointments have been placed on the schedule, take the remaining items on your list and transfer them, one by one, to the schedule, allotting adequate time to accomplish each of them. Transfer your top priority items first, then your high priorities, then your medium priorities, and, finally, transfer the low priority items, providing there is still time left on your schedule. Be sure to stop entering activities when there is still an hour or so left in each day. This will give you time slots into which to displace planned activities when unexpected ones arise. When your dotted-line appointments come up on the priority list, confirm these on your schedule by filling in the dotted lines.

Some Additional Tips

It is a good idea to place higher priority items toward the beginning of the week so that, if these take longer than you expected, you will still stand a good chance of getting them done.

To schedule very brief activities such as phone calls, letters, small errands, etc., simply list these out in some blank space at the bottom of whichever day seems best suited for them. You can also use this space to write out brief messages you want to cover in a meeting, etc.

If you have completely filled out your schedule and find that five of your medium priority activities made the schedule and three of them didn't, compare the three that were left off with the five that made it to see if you would like to switch any of them. Take the slightly lower in priority medium activities off the schedule and replace them with slightly higher in priority medium activities.

As you are transferring your activities, don't forget to schedule your "personal well-being" priority, that is to say, be sure you are allowing yourself adequate time for sleep, meals and relaxation. Also be sure that you allow yourself adequate travel time. As your schedule is completed, you may even want to rearrange some of your activities in order to minimize travel. You will save valuable time by taking activities that are to be done in or near the same place and scheduling them together.

When you have completed your schedule, don't throw away your list of priority-ranked activities. You can use this as you schedule for following weeks, picking up those activities that you don't get done this week.

As you follow your schedule, it is a good idea occasionally to keep track of how much time you actually spend on your scheduled activities. This practice will help you to more accurately estimate the amount of time needed for these activities in the future.

The example that follows contains a sample of the kind of weekly schedule form which I use. Most office supply stores have several alternative weekly schedule books. If need be, create one that particularly suits you and have it printed.

By Way of Example

Let's look now at an example of how the steps we have just discussed actually applied to the scheduling of a week:

1. List Activities: On Saturday morning, February 10, John Morton had a time of prayer with the Lord and proceeded to write his potential activities for the week of February 11-17. He came up with the following list:

POTENTIAL ACTIVITIES	John did not write out this column. Its purpose is merely to show you how John came up with his activities. The numbers correspond with the numbered activities listed under Step No. 1: List Activities in this chapter.
With God (devotions, church), family	1
Personal well-being (sleep, meals, exercise, etc.)	2
Plan for following week	3
Talk to job applicants for full and part-time staff (complete initial hiring)	4—from yearly plan for his work and 7—from major work assignments
Train full and part-time interviewers (people to survey the community)	"
Oversee printing of questionnaire (Monday)	"
Arrange for questionnaires to be delivered to office (Wednesday)	"
Check on progress of computer program	"
Prepare for next week's orientation (7 hours)	"
Meet with supervisors to lay out the week and discuss problems	"
Prepare devotional talk for next week's prayer breakfast	4—from personal plan
Reading improvement program	"
Lunch meeting with Bob Mitchell—a local businessman (Thursday, 12-3 p.m.)	5—from pocket monthly calendar he carries
Meet with Reverend Carlson (Tuesday, 10-12 a.m.)	"

Meet with Reverend Taylor (Wednesday, 1-3 p.m.)
   "

Mid-week church services (Wednesday, 7-9 p.m.)
   6—regular weekly meetings

Businessmen's prayer breakfast (Tuesday, 7:30-8:30 a.m.)
   "

Go out witnessing—church calling program (Thursday, 7-9 p.m.)
   "

Evangelistic Bible study—including preparation and entertainment (Tuesday, 7-9 p.m.)
   "

Do this week's correspondence (2 hours)
   8—from secretary's calendar

Set up filing system (2 hours)
   "

Birthday party for Jim Foster (Monday, 7:30-9:30 p.m.)
   8—from wife's calendar

Dentist appointment (Saturday, 8-9 a.m.)
   "

Build bookshelves for basement workshop
   9—other items

Take car in for tune-up
   "

Look up Jim Clark (new businessman in town referred by a friend)
   "

John Jr.'s basketball game (Friday, 8-10 p.m.)
   "

Paint chair in the office
   "

2. Ask If Assignable: Next he asked if any of these were assignable to someone else. He concluded that he could assign the training of interviewers to Sam (one of his supervisors), the arranging for questionnaires to be delivered to Sue (his secretary), and taking the car in for a tune-up to Barb (his wife). He made the appropriate notation in front of each of these three activities.

3. Assess Priorities: Next John assessed the priorities of the remaining activities. When he had completed this step, his list looked like this:

POTENTIAL ACTIVITIES

T	With God (devotions, church), family
T	Personal well-being (sleep, meals, exercise, etc.)
H	Plan for following week
H	Talk to job applicants for full and part-time staff (complete initial hiring)
SAM	Train full and part-time interviewers (people to survey the community)
H	Oversee printing of questionnaire (Monday)
SUE	Arrange for questionnaires to be delivered to office (Wednesday)
H	Check on progress of computer program
H	Prepare for next week's orientation (7 hours)
H	Meet with supervisors to lay out the week and discuss problems
H	Prepare devotional talk for next week's prayer breakfast
M	Reading improvement program
M	Lunch meeting with Bob Mitchell—a local businessman (Thursday, 12-3 p.m.)
M	Meet with Reverend Carlson (Tuesday, 10-12 a.m.)
H	Meet with Reverend Taylor (Wednesday, 1-3 p.m.)
H	Mid-week church service (Wednesday, 7-9 p.m.)
H	Businessmen's prayer breakfast (Tuesday, 7:30-8:30 a.m.)
H	Go out witnessing—church calling program (Thursday, 7-9 p.m.)
H	Evangelistic Bible study—including preparation and entertainment (Tuesday, 7-9 p.m.)
H	Do this week's correspondence (2 hours)
M	Set up filing system (2 hours)
L	Birthday party for Jim Foster (Monday, 7:30-9:30 p.m.)
H	Dentist appointment (Saturday, 8-9 a.m.)
L	Build bookshelves for basement workshop
BARB	Take car in for tune-up
L	Look up Jim Clark (new businessman in town referred by a friend)
H	John Jr.'s basketball game (Friday, 8-10 p.m.)
L	Paint chair in the office

4. Schedule: Finally he placed the activities onto his weekly schedule. (To see what the completed schedule looked like, see the next page.)

The procedure John followed was as follows: First he placed his top and high priority, already-committed-to appointments onto the schedule (e.g., "Businessmen's prayer breakfast—Tuesday, 7:30-8:30 a.m."). Next he scheduled his medium and low priority appointments (e.g., "Meet with Rev. Carlson"—Tuesday, 10-12 a.m.) and placed dotted lines around these time slots. Next he entered the top priorities (e.g., "devotions," "church," "family," etc.). Then the high priorities were entered.

Then John entered the medium priorities until his schedule was completely filled except for the time left open for unexpected activities. He also confirmed the dotted line appointments. "Set up filing system" was the one medium priority activity left unscheduled. John felt he might be able to work this in during the "unexpected activities" time if other activities did not arise and he made a notation to that effect. He also made a note to himself that he would try to work in the "Build bookshelves" low priority activity during his family time as a family project. Some of the low priorities, however, just didn't make the schedule.

Notice on the schedule that John took care of the easier assignments by simply listing them as additional things to do. Since showing Sam how to train the interviewers will take a little time, John put it on Tuesday morning. Note travel time allowed between work and home.

SCHEDULE FOR WEEK OF: February 11-17

	SUN 11	MON 12	TUE 13	WED 14	THU 15	FRI 16	SAT 17
6	Exercise, shower, shave, etc. →						
7	Time with God (devotions) →						
8	Breakfast →		Prayer Breakfast	Breakfast →			
9	Family	Meet with supervisors	Show Sam how to train interviewers	Prepare for Orientation		This week's correspondence	Dentist Appt.
10							Plan for following week
11	Church	Oversee q'naire printing	Rev. Carlson	→		Talk to job applicants	Prepare devotional
12	Lunch →				Bob Mitchell	Lunch →	talk for next week
1	Family	Check on progress	Talk to job applicants	Rev. Taylor	(including lunch)	Talk to job	Family
2		of computer	applicants			applicants →	
3		program		Talk to job applicants		→	→
4	Time for unexpected activities →			→			
5	Travel home and relaxation →		Family and relaxation →	→			
6	Dinner →						
7		Family	Evangelistic	Mid-week	Calling	Family	
8	Church	→	Bible Study	church service	program	John Jr.'s	
9	Church			→		basketball game	
10	Reading improvement program →						
11	Sleep →						
12	→						
Add'l. Things To Do	Ask Barb to take car in for tune-up this week	Ask Sue to arrange for q'naire to be delivered Wed. Invite Jack to Bible Study	Try to set up the filing system in the time for unexpected activities if nothing else displaces it.				Perhaps make the bookshelves for the basement workshop. Family project. Play tennis with family

Introduction to
Chapters 11 through 17

The next seven chapters are intended to stimulate your thinking concerning needs you have in seven areas of life: spiritual, mental, physical, social, vocational, financial and family. The Scriptures tell us, "And Jesus kept increasing in wisdom and stature, and in favor with God and men" (Luke 2:52). This verse reveals that Jesus matured in four significant areas of His life: mental, physical, spiritual and social. These are four of the areas that we will take up. And since most of us have a vocation, or a primary way in which we spend our time, and a family, which involves a spouse and perhaps children, and since all of us receive and spend money in some way, we will also take up the areas of vocation, family and finances.

In each chapter the scriptural foundation is laid for the principles discussed in the area. In addition some analysis and structure is presented to provide a framework for your thinking. In no sense is the content presented exhaustive in detail on the areas or even the only way to think about the areas. At the end of each chapter there is a list of additional resource material.

The main point of each chapter is to cause you to think. Perhaps you will see some aspect of each area that has never occurred to you before, but is conceivably a need in your life.

As you read through the chapters, it would be a good idea to have a pad of paper and a pen or pencil at hand so that, when you perceive an area in your life that needs improvement, you can make a note of it. Before you begin each chapter, ask God for the wisdom to know which of the ideas discussed He would have you concentrate on developing in your life.

I might caution you not to note every single new thought that occurs to you. Simply write down what stands out to you that God is especially impressing on you to apply.

When you have finished all seven chapters, save your notes. Then, the next time you set six-to-twelve-month objectives for yourself, bring them out. They will be most useful in reminding you of the areas in which you need improvement. It is quite possible your number one objective will come from these notes. After this next planning session, keep saving the notes for subsequent sessions.

11

The Spiritual Area of Life

The spiritual area of life has to do with our relationship with God and is therefore the most important area of all.

In Chapter 2 we discussed how you can walk with God and how that walk is key to managing yourself in the best way possible. By maintaining a close walk with God, you are able to receive His wisdom and be empowered to experience the character qualities of life He intends for you to have. You learned that walking with God does not insure that the circumstances of your life will be free from care, but it does insure that your character will be increasingly conforming to the character of Christ. In Romans 8:29 we are promised that God fully intends to conform us to His image: "For whom He foreknew, He also predestined to become conformed to the image of His Son, that He might be the first-born among many brethren."

In the process of discipling new Christians over the years, we in the ministry of Campus Crusade for Christ have sought to determine from the Scriptures specific character qualities that would increasingly be true of a person if he were becoming conformed to the image of Christ. This chapter contains a list of such qualities.

Growing in these areas involves time, and it involves trusting God to cause progress. It is not achieved in a academic, uninvolved fashion. A disciple of Jesus Christ should seek to help develop a movement of Spirit-filled Christians who are obedient to God's Word and are actively involved in helping to fulfill the Great Commission. He should seek to associate himself with other disciples to accomplish this.

The most crucial quality in a disciple is *power* from God. This enables him to be sensitive to God moment by moment and to be able to fulfill what He asks him to do. Two other key qualities are *direction* and *action*. A disciple should be increasingly willing to follow the commands and principles of God's Word in his daily responses to God, others and himself. He should seek to be a person of action, willing to take the initiative not only in sharing the message of Christ with non-Christians, but also in ministering meaningfully and practically to fellow Christians.

The remainder of the chapter contains brief descriptions of 11 qualities that should increasingly exist in the life of a disciple.[1] Before you read through these descriptions, ask God for the wisdom to know which one or more of these qualities especially need to be further developed in your own life. Then be sure to make a note of these as you read.

Power

"But the fruit of the Spirit is love, joy, peace, patience, kindness, goodness, faithfulness, gentleness, self-control; against such things there is no law" (Galatians 5:22,23).

A disciple allows the Holy Spirit, who indwells him, to increasingly direct and empower his daily life. He is increasingly becoming aware of all that he is and has because of his relationship with Jesus Christ. Thus, he is becoming more and more conformed to the image of Christ.

---

[1]Earlier editions of *Managing Yourself* used the term "agape person" in this chapter. Later editions use the more common term "disciple."

Direction

"All Scripture is inspired by God and profitable for teaching, for reproof, for correction, for training in righteousness; that the man of God may be adequate, equipped for every good work" (II Timothy 3:16,17).

A disciple increasingly depends on the Word of God for direction and guidance in circumstances and accepts the Bible as his final authority—his source of knowledge about God, others and himself. He learns how to study the Word of God to understand properly its teachings and to apply these to his life and ministry.

Action

"Go therefore and make disciples of all the nations, baptizing them in the name of the Father and the Son and the Holy Spirit, teaching them to observe all that I commanded you; and lo, I am with you always, even to the end of the age" (Matthew 28:19,20).

Increasingly a disciple: 1) views his life as an opportunity to actively serve his Lord; 2) wins others to Christ; 3) helps to build them in their faith and, 4) sends them forth as spiritual multipliers to win and build others for the Savior. He seeks to live for Christ in his own sphere of influence, help fulfill the Great Commission in his generation and thus help change the world. He is prepared to serve God in the area of service to which God leads him.

Faith

"And without faith it is impossible to please Him, for he who comes to God must believe that He is, and that He is a rewarder of those who seek Him" (Hebrews 11:6).

A disciple is increasingly aware of the character of the triune God, that is to say, of the one God who is a person — Father, Son and Holy Spirit. He understands that faith is his proper response to all that God is and to all that He promises to those who trust and obey Him. Based on this understanding, he draws upon the infinite resources of God by faith in order to live the Christian life.

Stewardship

"And from everyone who has been given much shall much be required; and to whom they entrusted much, of him they will ask all the more" (Luke 12:48b).

A disciple seeks to allow Christ to be Lord of every area of his life, and that includes his mind, emotions, will, body, relationships, talents and material possessions. He recognizes that all he is and has is ultimately a gift of God, and he seeks to be a responsible steward of these blessings.

Prayer

"Pray without ceasing" (I Thessalonians 5:17).

A disciple, following the example of our Lord, His disciples and Christian leaders throughout the centuries, places a special priority on prayer in his daily life. He realizes that God delights in his fellowship, desires his worship and welcomes his requests. More and more He bears   before   God   in   prayer   those   to   whom   he   is ministering.

Obedience

"He who has My commandments, and keeps them, he it is who loves Me; and he who loves Me shall be loved by My Father, and I will love him, and will disclose Myself to him" (John 14:21).

A disciple seeks to obey God daily. As he understands the commands and desires of God, he grows in his willingness to submit to them and make them his own desires. He realizes that obedience to his heavenly Father involves submission to those in authority over him.

Love

"Beloved, let us love one another, for love is from God; and every one who loves is born of God and knows God. The one who does not love does not know God, for God is love"

(I John 4:7,8).

A disciple increasingly experiences the unconditional, supernatural love of God in his life and expresses that same love in meaningful ways to his family, friends and acquaintances—believers and non-believers alike.

Fellowship

"And let us consider how to stimulate one another to love and good deeds, not forsaking our own assembling together, as is the habit of some, but encouraging one another; and all the more, as you see the day drawing near" (Hebrews 10:24,25).

A disciple enjoys fellowship with God's people. He understands and is involved in the church both on a local and on a worldwide basis. He is also involved with and supports the church's effort to fulfill the Great Commission.

Vision

"But you shall receive power when the Holy Spirit has come upon you; and you shall be My witnesses both in Jerusalem, and in all Judea and Samaria, and even to the remotest part of the earth" (Acts 1:8).

More and more a disciple views the world, its problems, needs and opportunities from God's perspective. His prayer is, "Lord Jesus, if You were I, what would You be doing and planning in the power of the Holy Spirit?" He acknowledges that his talents, abilities and dreams are gifts from God and grows in his willingness to offer them back to the Lord Jesus Christ, trusting Him for their fulfillment.

Leadership

"To aspire to leadership is an honourable ambition" (I Timothy 3:1, New English Bible).

A disciple seeks to be a leader in the particular area in which God has placed him. As such, he encourages others to Christian commitment and Spirit-controlled action and words and mobilizes them in an ongoing movement to help fulfill the Great Commission.

These are the 11 qualities of life that characterize the individual who is becoming increasingly conformed to the image of Christ. As you read over these qualities, did you become aware of an area or areas in your spiritual life that particularly need improvement? Jot down your thoughts if you haven't already done so. Save your notes and add to them as you read the next six chapters.

Some Sources of Help

As you seek to trust God to develop these qualities in your life, don't forget that your pastor is your nearest source of information as to how you can do so. Ask him to recommend written materials or tapes that deal with the improvement areas God has impressed on you.

In addition, Campus Crusade for Christ has many materials that elaborate on the qualities we have discussed in this chapter and that point out ways you can develop them in your life. Just as an example, there are a number of booklets and Bible study materials that clearly explain how to let God's Spirit empower you as a Christian and give guidance to your life. To obtain these and other materials, or for further information, write: Campus Crusade for Christ, Arrowhead Springs, San Bernardino, CA 92414.

It would also be a good idea to stop by your local Christian bookstore and browse through the shelves that relate to your particular areas of need. Leaf through some of the books and read over the summaries on the back covers. Ask what the most popular materials are in your area of need. God has blessed the Christian world today with a large volume of very good material on many areas of the Christian life, and you would do well to make use of it.

FOR YOUR FURTHER STUDY

Bright, Bill. Transferable Concepts Series. San Bernardino, California: Campus Crusade for Christ, 1971.

Chambers, Oswald. *My Utmost for His Highest*. New York: Dodd, Mead and Company, 1935.

Cowan, Charles E. *Streams in the Desert*. Grand Rapids: Zondervan Publishing House, 1965.

Murray, Andrew. *God's Best Secrets*. Grand Rapids: Zondervan Publishing House, 1957.

Schaeffer, Francis. *How Should We Then Live?* Old Tappan, New Jersey: Fleming H. Revell Co., 1976.

Smith, Hannah W. *The Christian's Secret of a Happy Life*. Old Tappan, New Jersey: Fleming H. Revell Co., 1968.

Tozer, A. W. *Knowledge of the Holy*. New York: Harper & Row, Publishers, Inc., 1961.

12

The Mental Area of Life

The mental area of life is very important. Proverbs 23:7 teaches that it is what a person thinks within himself that is a true indicator of what kind of person he is. In the privacy of our thought lives, we reflect our true selves, free from the constraints of pleasing the people around us.

It is through the mechanism of the mind that God transforms us into the people He wants us to be. Romans 12:2 tells us, "And do not be conformed to this world, but be transformed by the renewing of your mind, that you may prove what the will of God is, that which is good and acceptable and perfect." And in Ephesians 4:23,24, we find, "And that you be renewed in the spirit of your mind, and put on the new self, which in the likeness of God has been created in righteousness and holiness of the truth."

There is a great blessing in having our minds filled with the knowledge and wisdom of God. Proverbs 3:13-26 describes this blessing as being better than silver and gold and as including, among other things, long life, riches and honor, peace, happiness, security and freedom from stumbling.

II Peter 1:5-8 lists knowledge as one of the steps in a

sequence that leads to a mature relationship with Christ.
Contrast this with the "rewards" of a depraved mind:

> And just as they did not see fit to acknowledge
> God any longer, God gave them over to a de-
> praved mind, to do those things which are not
> proper, being filled with all unrighteousness,
> wickedness, greed, malice; full of envy, murder,
> strife, deceit, malice; they are gossips, slander-
> ers, haters of God, insolent, arrogant, boastful,
> inventors of evil, disobedient to parents, without
> understanding, untrustworthy, unloving, unmer-
> ciful (Romans 1:28-31).

Fortunately, as we walk with God we have access to
knowledge of the truth. In fact, in John 14:6 we learn that
Jesus is the actual embodiment of truth. Consider, too, the
following related passages: "The fear of the Lord is the
beginning of knowledge . . . " (Proverbs 1:7). And "The
testimony of the Lord is sure, making wise the simple. The
precepts of the Lord are right, rejoicing the heart; The commandment of the Lord is pure, enlightening the eyes" (from
Psalms 19:7,8).

With such wonderful promises as these, our challenge is
to learn how to be better stewards of the mental areas of
our lives and to capitalize fully on God's many blessings.

The Mental Functions and God's Guidance

Let us determine, then, just how we can go about becoming better stewards of our minds. Perhaps the best approach
is to examine carefully the various functions of the mind.
As we understand how these operate, we will be specifically
equipped to seek mental improvement. A simplified view of
the mental functions is that they involve three kinds of
activity: receiving, processing and sending. "Receiving" includes seeing, hearing, touching, etc. "Processing" includes
interpreting, storing in memory, deciding, etc. "Sending"
includes talking, writing, gesturing, etc.

In order to experience God's blessings we need to allow

Him to be present and give guidance in each function. For example, our receiving should be heavily saturated with the Word of God and with other edifying kinds of information. By the same token, we should avoid receiving those things which might cause us to sin.

As we process the information that enters our minds, we should consider how it relates to God's Word and pray for God's wisdom to interpret it properly.

As for our memories, we should be selective as to what we put there, choosing those things that are honoring to God.

Before we speak or act, we should be certain that such mental output is in accordance with the tenents of Scripture. That is to say, everything we say or do should be done to the glory of God and to the edification of those around us.

Pause for a moment and ask yourself if God is in control of all aspects of the mental area of your life. If He isn't and you want Him to be, pray and ask Him to guide your mind.

The Mental Function of Receiving

Now let's consider the mental function of receiving information. As we begin, be sure to have your note pad out, looking for points that are especially applicable to you.

The majority of information we receive comes to us by way of our five basic physical senses: sight, hearing, touch, taste and smell. We also have a spiritual sense that brings us input from God.

We should constantly seek to develop our sensitivity to God so that we become increasingly receptive to His input into our lives. I suggest that you begin by asking God for an increased sensitivity to His Spirit.

We also should seek to improve our five senses if that is possible. Perhaps you need glasses, for example; good eyesight is too key to receiving information to leave it impaired.

Another improvement we should seek is to learn to read better and faster. We should be able to read 1,000 words per minute or more, and books and courses are available to help achieve that.

Learning to Observe

Most of us could benefit from increasing our powers of observation. We tend to reject a high percentage of the information that our five senses bring to us as we walk through life. Of course, some rejection is necessary, since we could not possibly use all the input we receive. And yet, careful, selective observation can bring us certain knowledge that is very useful.

One area in which most of us would benefit from increased powers of observation is in studying. Though we may be getting the general idea of what we read in the Bible, many of us are missing a great deal because we are not good studiers. We have not trained ourselves to observe specific word choices, grammar, context, etc.

Another area in which many of us are unobservant is in our conversations with others, and this often causes us to miss what they are really saying. It is not generally a person's words which reveal his frame of mind, but rather the subtleties of his tone of voice, his inflection, his expression, his choice of words, the pace at which he is speaking, and so forth. Though we usually notice the obvious extremes of joy, anger or deep sorrow, we often fail to perceive the evidence of such subtleties as minor disappointment or annoyance.

An example of not observing subtle non-verbal signals was evident in a friend's recounting of the night he proposed to a certain young woman. Her response started with a long pause, then the word "well," then another long pause, and finally a very weak "yes," accompanied by a concerned look. Now my friend thought that reply to be an unqualified acceptance, and he began to make plans and tell others of his good fortune, only to have his would-be bride break off the engagement in a matter of weeks. For, you see, she had never totally agreed to marry him. Now, the story has a happy ending in that the couple did eventually marry, but my friend could have saved himself and his future bride much embarrassment had he not allowed his initial enthusiasm and hope and expectation to overrule his powers of observation.

Maintaining Three Key Attitudes

As you work on developing your powers of observation, there are three basic attitudes you should seek to maintain: inquisitiveness, alertness and awareness.

First, inquisitiveness involves the continual asking of questions. Let me hasten to say here that I am not suggesting that you become a "nosy" person, known for your lack of tact! No, the Bible has plenty to say against gossip and undue interest in the personal lives of others. What I do mean, however, is that, when you come across something out of the ordinary, question it. For example, I remember one time while on a trip, my wife and I passed a hillside that had a very unusual formation of stones and no vegetation whatsoever. We spent a good deal of time simply trying to imagine how such a phenomenon would have occurred.

When someone explains a new concept to you, don't stop with the first explanation; probe more deeply and see if you can't learn more about what is being shared. A side benefit of this practice is that you will be expressing a sincere interest in the person who is sharing with you. The primary benefit is that you will be enlarging your knowledge.

To keep your mind functioning at top capacity, take on some of the characteristics of a good reporter. Keep yourself alert and constantly ask what, where, how, why, when and who.

Second, alertness involves being "tuned in" to what's going on around us. I am thoroughly convinced that most people go through life in some sort of sleep-like or trance-like state and are anything but tuned in. "Apathetic" describes many people, as opposed to "motivated" and "interested."

To help guard against this situation in my own life, I like to work at a stand-up desk. When people ask me why I do this, my response is simple: "I have yet to fall asleep standing up." Life is too short and I have far too much to do to spend my afternoon half-dozing after a big lunch. Therefore, to stay alert I stand up or walk around in my office.

By way of contrast, I sometimes look around the room in an afternoon meeting and can tell very quickly that the average person in that room is not alert.

Third, awareness involves absorbing information in a variety of fields. The world is not so simple that it can be understood in the context of any single discipline of knowledge. A person can have a doctor's degree in physics and still be terribly ignorant of what is going on around him unless he makes an effort to add a certain amount of breadth to his knowledge.

Make it a habit to skim a newspaper or listen to an all-news station daily. From time to time leaf through a magazine or book on a subject totally new and different to you. Occasionally participate in some new activity. All these things give you a broader base of information from which to draw for sounder judgment in decision-making and for relating better to people.

I once read an article about how a well-known coach for a Big Ten conference football team, conducted himself while in the home of a young man he was seeking to recruit. What particularly impressed the parents about him was that he was interested in a wide variety of things, including them as people, rather than being single-minded about college football. They could envision him helping their son become a well-rounded individual, in addition to a better football player.

Paul tells us in I Corinthians 9:19-23 that he has become "all things to all men" so that he might fully accomplish the objective that God has given him. Paul recognized the value of keeping up with many things, not just those within his own personal sphere of interest, and so should we.

How well do you receive information? If there is a major

way in which you could improve, note it for future reference.

The Mental Function of Processing

More could be said about this function of the mind than about either of the others, and yet space does not allow. Therefore, let me merely stimulate your thinking about this function by bringing to your attention some of the processes your mind must go through day in and day out, and then challenge you to determine if these processes are carried out as well as they could be in your own mind.

Memorizing

When any piece of information is picked up by one of your senses, you are immediately faced with a choice as to what to do with that information: You can either act upon it, store it in your memory or discard it altogether.

Let's talk for a minute about memory. Storing something in your memory bank usually involves a definite thought process. Consistently, my most embarrasing moments are when a person has just told me his name and I promptly, totally forget it. In fact, I find that, if I do not think about and repeat a name several times during the next few seconds after I hear it, then I will tend not to remember it at all.

The most common helpful suggestions found in books on the subject of memorizing include: Associate a new fact with one that you already know very well, exaggerate or distort your mental image to help you visualize a new fact, create motion in your mental image. All these techniques cause you to create a vivid visualization in your mind which is difficult to erase.

Forgetting

Perhaps equally important, if not more important, than learning how to remember is learning how to forget. Of course, we are all able to forget things quite naturally; unfortunately, however, we are not very selective in the process. All too often we forget those things which we really need to remember, and remember those things which we would have done well to forget.

Of all the mental skills I have been working on in recent years, the one that has helped me as much as any other is this particular skill of discarding what I do not need to remember. My responsibilities often require that I hold or attend seven or eight meetings per day. In order to focus on the events of the meeting at hand, I must be able to clear my mind of whatever was discussed at the previous meetings. The only way I can do this and still keep on top of my responsibilities is to write down everything that I need to retain or act on from each meeting before it is over. By depending on a written system rather than on my memory to record all of the little odds and ends that must be seen to in the course of the day, the majority of my mind is left free to focus on whatever it is that is presently being discussed or whatever project I am currently working on.

The procedure for not remembering is just the opposite of that for remembering. Therefore to forget, don't repeat, associate, exaggerate, etc.

Interpreting

The minute a piece of information enters our brains, we tend to interpret it, that is, form an opinion with regard to it. How well we do this depends partly on the quality and quantity of our past experience in thinking about similar kinds of information. The more varied and developed our past experience, the more accurate our interpretation of new data based on that experience. Also, in coming to a conclusion, common sense is key.

To better understand this process of interpretation, let's apply it for a moment to a verse of Scripture. A good choice for our purposes would be Matthew 5:13: "You (Christians) are the salt of the earth."

Unless we conclude Jesus is saying that we are small grains

of a translucent mineral substance, we must assume that His words are to be interpreted figuratively. In the context of the Beatitudes, which immediately precede this verse, I think that a more logical interpretation of "salt" would be as a symbol of our distinctiveness as Christians. Our lives are to have a holiness that cannot be found in the life of the non-believer.

To see how this is so, that is, to build on our interpretation, we need to look to our understanding of the characteristics of salt itself. For one thing, salt has the capacity to flavor our food. In like manner, we as Christians have the capacity to flavor the world, that is, to make it more tasty or palatable to God and to man. In addition, salt makes people thirsty for water. In like manner, we as Christians can make people thirsty for the living, spiritual water, or God. Salt can also be used to clear a path, a fact alluded to in the passage itself. We as Christians are used to clear a path to God.

There are many more parallels that can be drawn here. What I want you to see is that, the greater your familiarity with the characteristics of salt, the more parallels you will find. In other words, the more varied and developed your past experience, the more adept you will be at the business of interpreting new data.

Applying

Applying involves connecting of new learning to our own situations. Some of us do this too much, and others too little. For example, some people take everything they hear personally when they should not be so sensitive. Others never even apply the most obviously needful lessons.

Good application, then, begins with the good judgment to select from all new information what is worth applying personally and involves coming up with ways to implement that new idea.

Conceptualizing

Conceptualizing involves receiving information, comparing it to facts in memory, and seeing patterns and relationships in all these facts. This process normally leads to a simplified organization of the facts which is more useful than are the many facts taken at random.

One good way to test your skills at conceptualizing and correlating is to try to anticipate what a person will say next after you have been talking with him for a few minutes, or to try to determine what the next thought will be after you have been reading for awhile. If, in fact, you are good at recognizing patterns, you should be quite adept at this.

Planning

Planning is a mental function that is a part of every day, if not a part of every hour. When we start most activities, we normally look at least a little ahead in time. I will not elaborate on this process here since we talked about the "how to's" of planning in a previous chapter.

Decision-making and Problem-solving

Decision-making and problem-solving are related processes that we go through from morning until evening every day of our lives. Take the very act of dressing, for example. When a man gets to his closet in the morning, he may first decide what shirt he is going to wear. This might involve choosing from among many different alternatives. Next he decides what slacks to wear with the shirt he has chosen. Then he may decide if he is going to wear a tie, and if so, what tie would look best. At any juncture, if something is not clean, then he may have to start the process all over again.

I have found the word "problem" to be one of the most common words I hear. People often describe their situations with an introduction such as, "The problem with this is . . . " or "My problem is . . . "

Unfortunately most people have never learned much about how to make decisions or solve problems. That is probably acceptable for less consequential decisions and problems, but for more significant ones, it is probably not acceptable. Decision-making and problem-solving are learnable skills.

Meditating

Meditating involves allowing our minds to dwell on or mull over certain thoughts so that they really penetrate into our memories and into our daily lives. These days a Christian is exposed to a great deal of wrong information on this subject from proponents of eastern religions. However, the Bible does encourage us to meditate on the right things:

Finally, brethren, whatever is true, whatever is honorable, whatever is right, whatever is pure, whatever is lovely, whatever is of good repute, if there is any excellence and if anything worthy of praise, let your mind dwell on these things (Philippians 4:8).

How blessed is the man who does not walk in the counsel of the wicked, nor stand in the path of sinners, nor sit in the seat of scoffers! But his delight is in the law of the Lord, and in His law he meditates day and night (Psalms 1:1,2).

Praying

Perhaps the most important mental process of all involves our prayer lives. We are invited in Scripture to pray about everything. Philippians 4:6,7 admonishes us, "Be anxious for nothing, but in everything by prayer and supplication with thanksgiving let your requests be made known to God. And the peace of God, which surpasses all comprehension, shall guard your hearts and your minds in Christ Jesus."

In I Thessalonians 5:17 we are told to "pray without ceasing." I used to puzzle over how that was possible until I began to realize how our minds operate. We can focus wholeheartedly on any one thing for only so long before our minds drift on to something else. In addition, we tend to respond in some way to most of the things that stimulate our five senses. The secret of praying without ceasing is to consciously involve God in our thoughts at every opportunity. When our minds begin to drift or when we start to respond to a stimulus, we can use those fleeting moments to address God, asking Him for wisdom or strength, thanking Him, rejoicing in Him, or whatever.

These specific parts of the processing function of our minds are only some of the more important ones. I hope, though, by considering these and how to improve your skills in doing them, you have been stimulated to think of some points that are especially valauble to you at this time. Before going on to the next section, you may want to note them.

The Mental Function of Sending

Our minds have the capability of sending information. Some of it is used internally to help us walk or sit, etc. Some of it is used to communicate with other people.

The communications we send may be very subtle and barely even consciously controlled, such as a raised eyebrow to indicate some question relative to a person's statement or action. Just as it is possible to learn to observe such signals, so it is also possible to learn to send them better.

Most of what we intend to communicate, though, is more obvious and conscious. Mainly we speak and write to communicate our thoughts. There is a great deal of help available to us in these two skill areas. The Dale Carnegie course, for example, is one of the oldest and most respected ways to learn how to speak in public. There are other materials on how to motivate people, how to speak in public, how to make yourself understood, how to write clearly, etc. If you sense a particular need to be more skillful in your speaking (public or private) and writing, seek out this help.

Let me share with you some general advice to supplement this. First, ask God to give you a special love for people.

"A new commandment I give to you, that you love one another, even as I have loved you, . . . By this all men will know you are My disciples . . . " (John 13:34,35). Jesus commanded us to love others at least partly, I'm sure, so that people could experience that love and respond more positively as a result of it. Even if you have to tell a person something unpleasant, he will accept it better if he knows you love him and want the best for him.

Second, be sure you are fully conforming to the standards of Scriptures in your communication. The Scriptures have a lot to say about what and how we communicate. For example, in Proverbs 15 we see that we should communicate gently, with a soothing tongue, with knowledge, without anger, on a timely basis, with pleasant and pure words, and with forethought.

Third, the following guidelines have been helpful to me in preparing talks and written materials.

1. Pray for wisdom.
2. Establish the objectives of your communication, that is to say, determine just what it is that you hope to communicate.
3. Determine the characteristics of the audience that will be receiving your communication.
4. Carefully come up with an outline or sequence of thoughts which would best convey your message to the audience that will be receiving it.
5. Seek to fill in your outline with specific illustrations and with other facts that would help communicate your ideas.
6. Be sure that you make clear what you are intending to communicate, both at the beginning and at the end of your presentation, and throughout your delivery as well.
7. Design a method of feedback to determine whether you have, in fact, succeeded in communicating what you intended.

Conclusion

In summary, we have discussed the importance of the mental area of life and of God's control in this area. We have considered various ways of improving our mental skills in receiving, processing and sending information. I am convinced that if our minds are functioning well, our lives will benefit greatly.

Perhaps as you have been reading this chapter, you have discovered something in the mental area of your life that you sense is a need. Be sure to note this before leaving this chapter.

FOR YOUR FURTHER STUDY

Adler, Mortimer J. and Van Doren, Charles. *How to Read a Book*. New York: Simon and Schuster, Inc., 1972.

Dale Carnegie Public Speaking Course. Carnegie Institution of Washington, Academic Press Inc., 111 Fifth Avenue, New York, New York 10003.

Hendricks, Howard G. "Communication," a cassette tape series. Here's Life Publishers, Campus Crusade for Christ, San Bernardino, California 92414.

Johnson, Ben E. *Rapid Reading with a Purpose*. Glendale, California: Regal Books Division, G/L Publications, 1973.

Kepner, Charles H. and Tregoe, B. B. *Rational Manager: A Systematic Approach to Problem Solving and Decision Making*. New York: McGraw-Hill Book Co., 1965.

Lucas, Jerry. *Remember the Word*. Los Angeles: Acton House, 1975.

Lucas, Jerry and Lorayne, Harry. *The Memory Book*. New York: Ballantine Books, 1974.

Morris, John O. *Make Yourself Clear! Morris on Business Communications*. New York: McGraw-Hill Book Co., 1972.

Richardson, H. Edward. *How to Think and Write*. Glenview, Illinois: Scott, Foresman & Co., 1971.

Strunk, William S., Jr. and White, E. B. *Elements of Style*, 2nd edition. New York: The Macmillan Co., 1972.

Wald, Oletta. *Joy of Discovery in Bible Study*, revised edition. Minneapolis: Augsburg Publishing House, 1975.

13

The Physical Area of Life

I think we would all agree that God is concerned with our spiritual maturity. But did you know that God is also concerned with the physical aspect of your life, that is to say, with your actual, physical body?

In I Corinthians 6:19,20, we are told that each of our bodies is "a temple of the Holy Spirit," and that each of us, having been purchased with a price (Christ's death on the cross), should now proceed to glorify God **in his body.** In Romans 12:1 we are further urged to present our **bodies** as a "living and holy sacrifice, acceptable to God."

Do you remember the parable of the talents in Matthew 25:14-30, which illustrates the principle that God expects us to be good stewards of whatever He has given us? How well this principle applies to our physical bodies which, like our time, our talents and our other resources, are gifts of God to be used for His glory!

In this chapter I would like to share with you 10 key principles that relate to the stewardship of our physical bodies or "temples." Craig Smith, a former staff member of Campus Crusade for Christ in San Bernardino, California, is the person who conceptualized most of these principles and I wish to hereby acknowledge his valuable contribution.

Pull out the paper on which you have been noting your improvement needs in the spiritual and mental areas of life. Pray that God will impress on you particular needs in the physical area of your life. As He does, add them to your overall list. Again, don't try to document every conceivable idea that is applicable to you. Just note the ones that you might be willing to consider as six-to-twelve-month objectives in the near future.

Principle No. 1: Believe That God Wants You to Be Healthy

It is natural for all of us to desire physical health with a body that is free of disease and functioning at its best. I personally believe that it is also God's desire that we be healthy; this was certainly part of His original plan for us before the Fall.

In III John 2, the following prayer is offered: "Beloved, I pray that in all respects you may prosper and be in good health, just as your soul prospers." And in John 10:10, Christ says: " . . . I came that they might have life, and might have it abundantly." Now the abundant life would seem to include our mental, emotional and spiritual health, which are far more significant than our physical health, but I think the abundant life could normally be interpreted to include our physical health as well. If that were not true, then why would Christ's ministry here on earth have so heavily emphasized the physical healing of the sick, and related that so closely to the spiritual principles of spiritual health as well?

Medical science is telling us these days that many of our bodily illnesses are really psychosomatic—that is to say, they are mind-induced or at least mind-assisted. Therefore, when we become exposed to a disease or when we think we might be coming down with one, our mental reaction to the situation might be a key to the outcome. There is nothing wrong with taking all reasonable medical precautions, but it would also be appropriate to claim God's basic intention that we be healthy and to pray for good health.

Of course, if we do become ill, we should not necessarily interpret this as an indication of our lack of trust in God. Many times God has some very worthwhile lessons to teach us in sickness. If we become ill, then the appropriate step is to fully receive and apply to our lives whatever it is that God wants to show us.

Principle No. 2: Enjoy Your New Life in Christ

Galatians 5:22,23 list the various parts of the fruit of the spirit. The first four of these are love, joy, peace and patience.

Think back in your own life to when you have abundantly experienced those qualities. Probably you can remember how good you felt physically in the context of great joy, say, or when you were experiencing great peace. When you ask people who are joyful how they are, they will generally say they feel good.

Consider Proverbs 14:30, which illustrates this phenomenon of the emotion of peace affecting physical health: "A tranquil heart is life to the body, but passion is rottenness to the bones." And consider Proverbs 17:22: "A joyful heart is good medicine, but a broken spirit dries up the bones."

In his book, *None of These Diseases*, Dr. S. I. MacMillen points out that worry is actually one of the primary causes of many of the diseases prevalent in America today.[1]

Principle No. 3: Confess Your Sins and Turn from Them

The Scriptures amply illustrate the adverse physical effects of failing to confess our sins and stubbornly refusing to turn from them.

---

[1] MacMillen, S. I. *None of These Diseases*. Old Tappan, New Jersey: Fleming H. Revell Co., 1963, pp. 61-62.

Consider Psalms 32:3,4: "When I kept silent about my sin, my body wasted away through my groaning all day long. For day and night Thy hand was heavy upon me; my vitality was drained away as with the fever-heat of summer."

Also consider Psalms 38:3-7: "There is no soundness in my flesh because of Thine indignation; there is no health in my bones because of my sin. For my iniquities are gone over my head; as a heavy burden they weigh too much for me. My wounds grow foul and fester. Because of my folly, I am bent over and greatly bowed down; I go mourning all day long. For my loins are filled with burning; and there is no soundness in my flesh."

The antidote to physical suffering caused by unconfessed sin is simply to confess the sin and turn from it, for, "If we confess our sins He is faithful and just to forgive us our sins and cleanse us from all unrighteousness" (I John 1:9). God's forgiveness releases us from feelings of guilt and thereby prompts physical health. In fact, David specifically observed this in Psalms 32:5: "I acknowledged my sin to Thee, and my iniquity I did not hide; I said, 'I will confess my transgressions to the Lord'; and Thou didst forgive the guilt of my sin."

Principle No. 4: Obey the Commands of Scripture

The Word of God is extremely powerful in combatting disease. In Exodus 15:26, the Lord promises "none of these diseases" to the Israelites if they will obey His commandments. Consider Proverbs 4:20-22: "My son, give attention to my words . . . for they are life to those who find them, and health to all their whole body." No doubt medical science will continue to find physical explanations for what techniques God uses to give us health as we follow His Word. In the meantime, though, I recommend you obey what the Bible prescribes for us.

Principle No. 5: Watch for Danger Signals

Automobiles often have red warning lights that signal to

us when something we cannot see is malfunctioning. God has wonderfully designed our bodies so that they, too, signal to us when they need special attention. Consistent dizzyness, nausea and pain in a specific area in the body are all examples of the danger signals that God allows our bodies to give us.

Sometimes when a danger signal occurs, we may be aware of a possible cause. For example, if we feel sluggish and we haven't been getting much sleep, we should try getting to bed earlier. If our efforts don't help and the danger signal persists, we should consult a doctor. After all, we would do at least as much for our car by taking it to a mechanic if it malfunctioned in some way!

In addition to consulting a doctor when a danger signal occurs, I heartily recommend a regular physical check-up as a preventive measure. For some years now, I have had a complete physical every year. The detailed advice that I have received from the doctor, nutritionist and others involved with the physical has no doubt prevented many problems for me in the past and will certainly prevent many more problems in the future—problems that might be very difficult to cure if allowed to develop. The advantage of a physical is that early warning signals can be detected long before your body gives you a more obvious signal of the problem.

Principle No. 6: Control the Quality of Your Food Intake

Sound eating habits are directly beneficial to physical health. For example, that is probably one reason the Israelites were warned about eating the fat of animals (Leviticus 3:17). Daniel illustrates the superiority of vegetables and water over rich food (Daniel 1:12-15).

Each of us needs to prayerfully study what qualified nutritionists have to say concerning the food we eat, and then we should apply the advice to our own diets. The following are some points which many experts recommend:

1. Eat a balanced diet from the basic food groups: milk

and other dairy products, meat, fruits and vegetables, grains and breads. Candy and other highly processed snacks are poor substitutes for this balance.

2. Greatly reduce your refined sugar intake and cut back some on your meat consumption. Most Americans consume far too much sugar and probably too much meat for optimum health.

3. Eat your food closer to the state in which God originally created it rather than in a highly altered form. For example, raw vegetables or those which have been lightly cooked are generally superior in nutritional value to highly cooked or processed vegeables.

4. Eliminate the use of beverages which contain caffeine or alcohol. There are several healthy alternatives you can drink, such as herb tea, Postum and other types of grain-based beverages.

Principle No. 7: Control the Quantity of Your Food Intake

It has been said that we are largely what we eat; I might add that some of us are more largely what we eat than others! In Philippians 3:19 we see overeating and other overindulgences as a bad thing, because they set up food and other earthly pleasures as gods which we worship. In I Corinthians 9:24-27 we see the principles of keeping our bodily desires under control for the sake of a more important objective. Medical science has given us plenty of reason to believe that being overweight can be a primary cause of many diseases and leads to serious complications in others. Therefore, if we are to be good stewards of our bodies, we must eat in moderation to keep our weight in proportion to our height and bone structure.

I find I can curb my appetite by drinking a lot of water. However, there are many books, courses, even whole institutes whose aim is to teach you how to diet, so I won't begin to deal with that subject here. Whatever diet method you choose, the key to success will be for you to trust God for the discipline to stick to it.

Principle No. 8: Exercise Regularly

In I Timothy 4:8, Paul says that bodily exercise profits us a little though there are other things that profit us even more. Now Paul was speaking to a society which was physically very active and in which almost everything was done by hand. The American society, however, is quite sedentary, and much of the heavy work is done by machine. Our bodies are designed for a much higher level of physical activity than we are normally afforded in the course of our daily lives. Therefore, most Americans need to supplement their normal activities with exercise.

There are many types of exercise from which to choose: walking, swimming, jogging, bicycle riding, or whatever else appeals to you. But whatever you choose, be sure that it is practical for you and is something you will be motivated to do day in and day out. The two activities that I can do most often and most easily are jumping rope and jogging. I can personally attest to the fact that since I first incorporated these into a regular exercise program a couple of years ago, I have felt more alert, more in shape and more comfortable with the various demands on me than ever before.

Principle No. 9: Seek Proper Rest and Sleep

In Psalms 127:2 we are told, "It is vain for you to rise up early, to retire late, to eat the bread of painful labors; for He gives to His beloved even in his sleep." In Mark 6:30-32 Jesus advises His disciples to take some special time just to rest. What about your own lifestyle? Are you "eating the bread of painful labors"? Do you need to take time out to rest?

People seem to vary as to the amount of sleep they need at night. But whatever the right amount is for you, your health demands that you get it. Generally speaking, it is better to go to bed at the same time each evening and wake up at the same time every morning. Your body will become accustomed to the schedule and will be ready to rest fully at the given time.

In addition to a good night's sleep, you may need to have a time during the day when you can take a break from whatever you've been working on, put up your feet, and just relax for a while.

Principle No. 10: Take Care of Your Appearance

One of the characterisitics God has given you physically is your appearance. The exterior of your "temple of the Holy Spirit" (I Corinthians 6:19) is important, too. Study some time the quality and beauty of material and the skillfulness of workmanship that went into building God's temple in Solomon's time (I Kings 5-7).

I know of many people who have become lax in taking care of their appearances and as a result suffer a tremendous lack of confidence and a corresponding depreciation in their abilities to function well with other people. If people are tremendously overweight, for example, they often don't enjoy mixing with people socially because they are embarrassed. This condition is frequently worsened by the principle mentioned in Proverbs 23:7: "For as he thinks within himself, so he is." A little lack of confidence breeds even more of a lack.

A person will find it more difficult to step out and aggressively minister for God if he is not sure that he is an appropriate representative of God. Therefore, seek to honor and glorify God in your appearance just as you would seek to in other areas.

Conclusion

As you endeavor to improve the physical aspect of your life to the glory of God, you will probably feel better and look better than you ever have before. And you will probably live longer. Blake Clark, in a February, 1976, *Reader's Digest* article, reported on a survey to determine the secret of several hundred Americans who lived to be a hundred or more. Among the characteristics of these people were eating the right foods, freedom from worry, adequate sleep, a cheerful disposition and strong religious convictions—the very things we've been talking about!

Before leaving this chapter, be sure to note the most significant ways you could improve the physical area of your life.

FOR YOUR FURTHER STUDY

Carlson, Dwight L. *Run and Not Be Weary.* Old Tappan, New Jersey: Fleming H. Revell Co., 1974.

Cavanaugh, Joan. *More of Jesus, Less of Me.* Plainfield, New Jersey: Logos International.

Cooper, Kenneth H. *The New Aerobics.* New York: Bantam Books, 1970.

Josephson, Elmer A. *God's Key to Health and Happiness.* Old Tappan, New Jersey: Fleming H. Revell Co., 1962-1976.

MacMillen, S. I. *None of These Diseases.* Old Tappan, New Jersey: Fleming H. Revell Co., 1963.

Rohrer, Norman and Virginia. *How to Eat Right and Feel Great.* Wheaton: Tyndale House Publishers, 1977.

14

The Social Area of Life

The social area of life concerns our relationships with other people. Luke 2:52 records that Jesus grew in favor with men as well as with God. As a social being, He related well to those around Him, and so should we. Throughout the Bible great attention is given to telling us how we should treat other people. The last six of the Ten Commandments, for example, tell us to honor our parents, not to take our neighbor's life, wife, material goods or reputation, and not to even think about possessing what is our neighbor's.

In addition to prescribing how to relate, the Scriptures encourage us to relate to other people. For example, we are to **avoid** the "forsaking (of) our own assembling together" (Hebrews 10:25); that is to say, we are to have fellowship with other Christians. The apostle John knew the value of fellowship. In I John 1:3 he reveals that one of the reasons he wrote that epistle and proclaimed the message of Christ was "that you also may have **fellowship** with us; and indeed our fellowship is with the Father, and with His Son Jesus Christ" (emphasis mine).

An Influence for Good

As part of our fellowship, we are to "stimulate one another to love and good deeds" (Hebrews 10:24), and to "encourage one another day after day" (Hebrews 3:13). In short,
we are to influence each other for good. We are also to learn
to regard one another as more important than ourselves
(Philippians 2:3), a point of view that is only possible as we
are walking in the Spirit.

Paul suggests in Philippians 2:1-4 that fellowship of this
variety helps to promote a wonderful unity of mind, love and
spirit among believers. The Greek word used for "fellowship"
in I John 1 has as its root the word which means "common."
Christian fellowship is to have an "in commonness" or unity
about it. Jesus sought such unity for his own disciples, and
prayed that "they may all be one . . . " (John 17:21). For
one thing, He knew that the world would take note of a message whose adherents were actually at one with each other,
because that would be so different from normal.

An Adverse Influence

Just as we can be influenced for good through a fellowship that is honoring to God, so can we be adversely influenced by people who are not walking with God. That is why
Proverbs 1:15 admonishes us not to "walk in the way with
them" (sinners), but to "keep (our) feet from their path."

Psalms 1:1 tells us that we are blessed when we do not
associate with the wicked, with sinners or with scoffers.
In I Corinthians 5:9-13, Paul instructs the church at Corinth
not to associate with people who claim to be Christians but
really lead immoral lives. All these warnings stem from the
fact that the bad habits of our friends tend to rub off on us.

The story of the Good Samaritan and the example of the
life of Christ make clear, however, that we are not to snub
people. We are to love, be genuinely interested in and seek to
minister to anyone. The above Scriptures simply seem to be
warning us not to seek to have hardened, unrighteous people

as our primary, close friends, who are most influential on our walk with God.

Let's look now at the various levels of relationship we generally experience in our lifetimes and think about how we can best achieve God's purpose in each of them. As always, pray for God's wisdom as you approach this subject, be on the lookout for concepts that are particularly helpful to you, and write them down.

Definition of Levels of Relationship

To help our thinking, I would like to categorize our social relationships into four groupings: family, close friends, acquaintances and other friends, and strangers. Let me define the terms.

First, the naturally closest relationship we normally have is with our immediate family. Our first relationships of any sort are normally with our parents, brothers and sisters. Later, we normally form relationships with the life-mates that God gives us and with our children.

Second, most of us form some close friendships. These are with people we especially enjoy and, therefore, with whom we tend to spend a fair amount of time. Their life-styles and attitudes tend to have a significant impact on us and vice versa.

Third, there is a less close group of friends and acquaintances. We "know" them and are "friendly" to them, but we don't tend to confide in them a great deal or spend a lot of social time with them. Many work, church, club and neighborhood relationships are in this category.

Fourth, when we first meet someone, that person is basically a stranger to us. We most likely don't know anything about him at first.

Now I would like for us to think together about our objectives and activities with regard to these different types of relationships we tend to form. How can the social area of life best fit into our overall objective of glorifying God?

My experience has shown me that there is a wide variation

in the amount and type of social life to which God calls different people. Whereas the principles of relating to our family are fairly prescribed by the Scriptures, God seems to allow a fairly wide variation in the number and closeness of our friendships, apparently depending on our callings in life. John the Baptist would be on the low extreme, and probably Barnabas would be on the high side in terms of numbers of friends.

Therefore, I would like for the following discussion to stimulate you to prayerfully consider what God has specifically called you to do in the social area of your life.

Family

Since family relationships are so important, I have devoted Chapter 17 to that subject rather than cover it more briefly here. So let's move on to the next level of relationship, close friends.

Close Friends

First of all, who are your close friends? All too often our close friends have not been chosen; they have **happened** to us. Sometimes they are the very ones God would have for us, but other times they do not really meet the normal qualifications of "close friend." The closer a person is to us, the more impact he tends to have on our lives. If we are primarily close to people who do not seek to honor God in their daily lives, we will tend to be drawn away from God by them.

Take the time to prayerfully consider who it is that God would have as your close friends. Ask Him if any of your close friends have become a hindrance to your spiritual life. Discern which of your close friends are really helping you in your walk with God.

If someone is a bad influence on you, first try to think of ways you can minister to that person to cause his life to come closer to the standards of the Scriptures. Also try to think of ways to communicate to him how important it is to you to glorify God with your life, without sounding "holier than Thou." If he is not responsive or understanding and if God seems to be leading you to cool down the friendship some, try to think of ways you can continue to show your love and concern for him and minister to him without incurring negative influence on your life.

Is there someone new to whom God seems to be leading you to become close? Of course, you don't have enough time to be best friends with everybody, but God may be opening a new door.

Once you know who your close friends are supposed to be, commit yourself to them. Take the initiative to cultivate the relationship. Invite them to dinner, talk with them on the phone, share prayer requests, attend mutually interesting activities. Involve them with your family, and be involved with theirs.

Do be careful, however, that your closest friends don't become your **exclusive** friends. Remember that, although Jesus was close to His disciples, and especially close to three of them, His ministry took in multitudes of acquaintances and strangers as well.

As you spend time with your close friends, ask yourself what they might know that would really minister to your life, and then stimulate the conversation along these lines. Also bring up those things from your own experience which you feel might be useful to them. Look for a wide variety of ways to express your love for your friends and then do so, often. And be open to their doing the same thing in your behalf. Pray often for them.

Acquaintances and Other Friends

Almost all of us have a large number of people in this category. There may be a number of reasons God brought them into your life. Two of these reasons are for you to minister to them and for them to minister to you.

See if you can think of ways for these two objectives to be accomplished in your less close friendships. Are you learning from them? What are their areas of particular strength? Are you being ministered to in these areas? Do they have needs in your particular area of strength? Are you seeking to minister to them? As you see God's purpose in your being together, can you think of specific ways you can achieve that purpose?

What about those among your acquaintances who are not strong believers or perhaps aren't even Christians? Here is a real opportunity for you to minister. Let God's love for them show in your actions and speech. Think of opportunities to seek to introduce them to Christ and/or increase their commitment to Christ. Seek to involve them with other people who can minister to them. Invite them to church or to a Bible study.

Be sure to live the Christian life before these people, trusting and obeying God. If they see something in your life that is better than what they are experiencing, you have their attention. If they don't see something better, your words are going to seem very hollow.

Strangers

The last level of relationship involves people we simply encounter in the course of life. We could call these people "strangers." Matthew 25:35-45 clearly shows us that strangers, too, should be treated with love and respect. We are encouraged to minister to their needs.

As we encounter people, we should seek God's purpose in bringing us together. Sometimes, for example, God intentionally places non-Christians in our path so that we might share with them His plan of love and forgiveness. Other times God brings into our lives believers who have a need in our area of special strength or experience. If we are sensitive to God's leading in these situations, He can use us to help meet such needs.

How do you react to people when you first meet them? Is your attitude toward them one of love and service? Are you sensitive to their needs? Do you seek to minister to them as the opportunity arises? Are you willing to learn from new people even as you first meet them? Are you open toward others and is your home open to those in need?

Do you feel that you are meeting enough new people? Could God be leading you to expand the number of people you meet in order to better achieve His purpose in your life? Remember that it is very easy to fall into the situation of knowing and meeting only other Christians. What activities do you participate in that enable you to meet a wide variety of people, including non-Christians?

One good way to meet new people is to take advantage of the natural social times in your life. For example, during your coffee or lunch break at work you have the opportunity to meet and talk to others. Pray for God's wisdom as to whom you should spend your time with. The same would apply to times before and after church, club and other activities.

Conclusion

God created us to be social beings. Ever since Eve joined Adam, man has had the opportunity for fellowship. Furthermore, our relationships with people tend to have great impact on our lives and vice versa. They are a major part of how God causes us to grow spiritually.

As you have read this chapter, have you seen some ways to improve the social area of your life? Are your relationships glorifying God to the maximum? Are you close friends with the right people? Are you seeking to minister to your acquaintances? Are you sensitive to the needs of even strangers?

Write down the areas in which you feel particularly led to act.

FOR YOUR FURTHER STUDY

Augsburger, David. *Caring Enough to Confront*. Glendale, California: Regal Books Division, G/L Publications, 1973.

Evangelistic Speaking and Entertaining. San Bernardino, California: Campus Crusade for Christ International, 1971.

Lewis, C. S. *The Four Loves*. New York: Harcourt Brace Jovanovich, Inc., 1960-1971.

Mains, Karen Burton. *Open Heart, Open Home*. Elgin, Illinois: David C. Cook, 1976.

Powell, John. *Why Am I Afraid to Tell You Who I Am?* Niles, Illinois: Argus Communications, 1969.

Tournier, Paul. *To Understand Each Other*. Atlanta: John Knox Press, 1967.

Wilson, Doug. *The Quest for Intimacy*. Santa Ana, California: Vision House, 1979.

15

The Vocational Area of Life

Most of us spend more of our waking hours pursuing a vocation than in any other single activity. And yet, more often than not, our vocations become fairly routine. We often become resigned to the traditional pattern of activities and don't think too much about why we are doing what we are doing. We don't always plan for our personal development in our careers and so we tend to drift in the current of opportunities that present themselves. This chapter should stimulate you to thought about you and your vocation. As with previous chapters, ask God for wisdom in discerning your areas of need, and then jot these down so that you will stand a better chance of implementing them.

Vocation Defined

Before we begin, let me define for you the scope of what I mean by "vocation" in this chapter. I am certainly including the making-of-a-living kind of pursuits like working on an assembly line, on a construction job, in an office situation or making calls in the business or residential community—in other words: job or ministry. I am also including the main activities of wives with children at home. Homemaking is every bit as much of a "vocation" as any of the other pursuits mentioned.

The Productive Life Is Scriptural

There is no doubt that to have a vocation is scriptural. The Bible clearly teaches that we are to lead active, productive lives as opposed to idle, non-productive ones. In the Old Testament, we find the statement, "Six days you shall labor . . . " (Exodus 20:9). Although the major point of this verse involves resting on the Sabbath, it does make clear that God intends for us to "labor."

In Proverbs 18:9, we are encouraged to work hard: "He also who is slack in his work is brother to him who destroys."

The New Testament is no easier on us. In II Thessalonians 3:10, Paul suggests to the church, "If anyone will not work, neither let him eat." In Romans 12:11, we are warned not to lag behind in diligence as we seek to function as part of the body of Christ.

As for the scriptural model for a wife's activities, consider the "excellent wife" described in Proverbs 31:10-31. Notice the number and quality of verbs just in the first few verses of that passage: "does," "looks," "works," "brings," "rises," "gives," "considers," "girds herself," "makes," etc.

Of course, busyness, in and of itself, does not achieve purpose, but it is clear that God intends for us to be active as we pursue our particular vocations, and as we seek to become increasingly conformed to the image of Christ.

The Elements of the Vocational Area of Life

There are some natural parts of our vocational development. First, we need to know what vocations God has called us to. Second, we normally need some sort of formal training. Third, in addition we normally require on-the-job experience to become proficient in our vocations. Fourth, we spend most of our years actually "producing" (working fruitfully). Fifth, through all of this, we need to continue to grow as people.

The rest of this chapter develops and helps you learn and apply these concepts.

Know Your Calling

The word "calling" refers to God's specific objective for an individual, particularly with regard to his vocation. As Christians, all of us are called equally to be conformed to the image of Christ (Romans 8:28-30). However, the Bible makes it clear that God also has a special calling for each one of us.

Consider, for example, Ephesians 2:10: "For we are His workmanship, created in Christ Jesus for good works, which God has prepared beforehand . . . . " And Psalms 139:16, in which the psalmist says to God, "Thine eyes have seen my unformed substance; and in Thy book they were all written, the days that were ordained for me, when as yet there was not one of them." Ephesians 14:6 refers to "the proper working of each individual part" of the body of Christ, suggesting that each of us has a specific function to perform. Though He may not choose to reveal the details of our callings all at once, the fact is that God does have a plan for our lives.

Some of us are quite sure of our calling from an early age. Others of us, pehaps the majority, need a little help in beginning to discover just what it is that God wants us to do. In Chapter 9, I shared with you several steps you might take to help you determine God's will. Here they are again in outline form:

1. Be sure you are filled with the Spirit (Ephesians 5:18; Proverbs 3:5,6).
2. Pray for specific wisdom (James 1:5-7).
3. Consider the scriptural objective common to all Christians (John 15:8)—to glorify God by:
   a. Being a disciple (becoming more Christ-like).

      b. Discipling other Christians.

      c. Sharing the gospel with non-Christians.

4. Consider Scriptures God has made particularly meaningful to you (II Timothy 3:16,17).

5. Consider key facts about yourself—gifts, specific interests, talents, past education and training, previous leading from God (Psalms 37:23).

6. Consider counsel (Proverbs 11:14).

7. Consider impressions (Philippians 2:13; John 10:27).

8. Compare the pros and cons of your various alternatives in light of the above (I Corinthians 2:15).

9. Ask God for His confirming peace (Colossians 3:15).

Read Chapter 9 for more detail on the points. Again, let me mention that just implementing the first point puts you a long distance in the direction of knowing God's will. Proverbs 3:6 tells us, "In all thy ways acknowledge Him, and He shall direct thy paths" (King James Bible). Now let's look at the second major aspect of your vocation—training.

Training Is a Must

The Old Testament books of Exodus, Leviticus, Numbers and Deuteronomy are chock-full of detailed instruction to the Israelites concerning their behavior in various situations, and Deuteronomy 6:6-9 cautions parents to make sure that their children remain continually aware of these instructions. God did not leave to chance the Israelites' understanding of **what** He wanted them to do and **how** they were to do it. In God's economy, anything worth doing is worth doing well.

This principle would certainly apply to your vocation, and to do it well, you will probably need some sort of training. For, although we may have the aptitude for an activity, we normally have to develop it to be really proficient. This principle is borne out in Exodus 35 and 36, which speak of men whose God-given skills were highly developed, qualifying them to participate in the building of the tabernacle.

Consider Your Options

In this day and age, some vocations have a program of training built right into the work itself. Most, however, require a certain amount of training before you arrive on the job. If you feel that God has called you to a vocation that calls for a formal training period, it would be wise to carefully examine each of your options before deciding on any particular college or other program. Consider the length, quality and expense of several good programs that would be open to you, and then determine which one is best suited to your own particular needs.

For example, if you are in your late fifties, an extended number of years spent in formal training for a new career might not be the most appropriate step. Or, if you are the provider for a family of four young children, you will probably not want to spend as much money on a training program as you would if you were single. The main thing is to be sure that the program you select is right for **you**.

Take Advantage of Your Training

Once you have begun a particular course of training, by all means work hard at it. Keep your objective in mind at all times. This, of course, is to learn as much as possible concerning your chosen vocation. I know many young people who waste much of their time in college. They appear not to realize or to have forgotten the primary reason they are there. This waste of time is usually regretted in later years.

Be aggressive in pursuing the knowledge you will need later. Reread Chapter 12 on the mental area of life to help you in this. Consider how what you are taught will apply to your future career, and how it applies to any past experiences you might have had. This will give you useful "hooks" on which to hang your knowledge, making it easier to remember and use later.

Don't Stop with Initial Training

Though the initial training period is invaluable, it is important to realize that vocational training should not end there. Throughout our lives we should seek to learn new concepts and update the ones we already know. We can attend seminars in our fields of interest, read trade and other magazines and take advantage of company-sponsored educational programs.

Homemaking Also Requires Training

Lest you think the only vocations that require training are career related, let me say that the principles we've discussed thus far could also be applied to homemaking. Unfortunately, however, many women become wives and mothers, make homemaking their primary career, and yet never seek formal, or even informal, training in the areas of cooking, housekeeping, raising children, ministering to a husband, etc. If you find yourself in this situation, or if any of these aspects of homemaking is particularly difficult for you, you will be glad to know that there are good books, tapes, seminars, etc., that deal with these subjects. By all means, take advantage of these resources.

In addition, young wives should seek to become close to women they respect who have greater experience in the realm of homemaking. Sometimes the skills in this area are best learned through observation and by way of advice. Titus 2:3-5 tells us that older women are to be respectable in their own behavior and then "teaching what is good" to the younger women, encouraging them "to love their husbands, to love their children, to be sensible, pure, workers at home, kind, being subject to their own husbands, that the word of God may not be dishonored."

Let us look now at the third major aspect of your vocation —experience.

Be an Apprentice

Much of what we learn about our vocations comes from

actual experience. One way to gain good experience is to select a few individuals with expertise in our field, and then watch those individuals carefully, day by day. This is very similar to the advice just given to homemakers, and is just as valid. Although formal apprenticeship is not as widespread today as it used to be, a modified apprenticeship situation can be very beneficial, especially as we begin our careers.

Take advantage of any opportunity to work with qualified people. Learn all that you can from them, both through careful observation and well-placed questions. If you can, apply what you learn to your specific job in order to consolidate what you are learning. Finally, ask about further resources, that is, find out what people, books, tapes, seminars, etc., they know of.

Seek Appropriate Employment

As you seek employment at the outset of your career, remember that these first work experiences, particularly, should prepare you for increased productivity in the future. Therefore, look for situations that will expose you to individuals with expertise in your field and that will really give you the experience you need. Look for jobs that will stretch you, and that will give you opportunities to sample a wide variety of experiences rather than confine you to a single main activity.

Let's look now at the fourth major aspect of your vocation—producing.

Production Is the Objective

When I was in college at MIT, I played basketball. In the winter, when it was cold outside, the crew team used to practice their sport on a walkway around the top of the gym where the basketball team worked out. While we were running around free and easy, dribbling and shooting, they were confined to strange devices designed especially for their use. These contraptions consisted of small sliding chairs and stubs of oars which were connected at one end to sludge pots. All evening long, the crew members slid back and forth in their chairs and pulled at their "oars," heating up the sludge in the pots. Not much of an accomplishment, or so it seemed.

When spring came, however, and the ice thawed on the Charles River, these same fellows could be seen on the water in their crew shells, eight to a boat plus a coxswain. The heavily muscled athletes strained at real oars now and handled them with skill, causing their boats to slice swiftly through the water.

I often share this story with young people to illustrate the fact that the training they are presently undergoing has as its purpose that someday they will put their oars in the water and cause some boat to move. The end result of training is doing.

Strive for Excellence

When we do arrive at the stage of production, it is not enough just to "do" in a half-hearted, sloppy manner. Consider Colossians 3:23,24: "Whatever you do, do your work heartily, as for the Lord rather than for men; knowing that from the Lord you will receive the reward of the inheritance. It is the Lord Christ whom you serve." And I Corinthians 10:31: "Whatever you do, do all to the glory of God."

Don't settle for mediocrity in your vocation. As a Christian, you march to the beat of a different drummer, so to speak, and you should strive for the excellence God has called you to.

Please note, however, that excellence is not the same as perfectionism. Perfectionism requires that a person do every single thing that can possibly be done in relation to a task. Excellence demands that the job be done very well, without wasting the resources God has given.

The Attitude of a Servant

Galatians 5:13 says that we are to "serve one another" through love. Therefore, as we are going about the business of producing, always striving for excellence, our attitude should not be one of pride, but should rather resemble that of a faithful servant.

All too often, however, we do our work zealously, even excellently, but with little or no regard for those around us, let alone any intention of serving them. Such a situation is never in accordance with God's will. We should seek to be sensitive to other people in the work situation, and look for ways that we can help or encourage them.

So far we have discussed the selection of your vocation (or the discovering of your calling), the preparation for your vocation (training and experience) and the actual pursuit of that vocation (production). Now let's look at the fifth and final aspect of the vocational area of your life—continued growth. The following are a number of thoughts on how to maximize personal growth in the context of vocation.

Be Willing to Stretch Yourself

Few if any people fully develop to their potential. There is almost always room for us to become better at whatever it is that we do. Training and experience both play a part in our improvement, but much of it simply comes from being willing to "stretch" ourselves, to go beyond what we have done before. All of us should seek to be stretched. Otherwise, we tend to stop thinking about what we are doing and become sloppy in our responsibilities. The desire to improve should accompany us all of our lives.

Be a Part of the Big Picture

None of us is really called to be a one-man show; we are all intended to fit into God's total plan, at work as well as in our churches and families. Therefore, instead of merely pursuing our own segments of the work load, we should seek to cooperate with other members of the work team, and fit into what they are doing; we should ask ourselves often, "How can I help to achieve the overall purpose here"? We are not just hammering nails—we are constructing buildings.

Keep Sight of the Objective

In the course of our work, God will allow many "opportunities" to cross our paths. We need to be alert to recognize the ones that contribute to our calling and take advantage of them. We need to be equally able to reject the dead-end streets. To discern the difference, we need to keep God's objective for our work firmly in mind and keep our minds thinking about the implications of what is happening around us.

All Works Together for Good

I once heard an old Chinese saying that went something like this: "When everything goes smoothly, the work grows; when everything is rough, you grow." As a Christian "who loves God and is called according to His purpose," you can welcome even adversity in your job because it is an opportunity for you to grow (Romans 8:28-30).

Be Sensitive to God's Continued Leading

When God first gave you an inclination as to your calling, He probably revealed only the barest outline for your life. He normally fills in that outline as time goes on. That being the case, it is very important that you remain sensitive and flexible to God's leading in your career so that you might know all He has for you.

Enjoy Your Vocation

Since we do spend so much time in the pursuit of our vocations, it would be a shame if we did not enjoy them. In

Chapter 5 I shared with you how God can motivate us to do whatever we must do and cause us to enjoy it in the process. Be sure not to miss out on claiming God's satisfaction for every activity that is part of your job, particularly when it is something that you do not naturally enjoy doing.

Enjoy Your Relationship with God

As a last point under "continued growth," I would simply like to say that, as you go about your vocation, don't forget to enjoy your relationship with God, to experience His joy and His peace and His love. And do not allow what you cannot get done in your job to put you under the pile. Remember that, at the time of His death, Jesus Christ was satisfied in the knowledge that He had glorified God, even though His active ministry lasted only three years, and much of the witnessing and discipling was left to posterity. Do pursue with zeal the opportunities that God places before you, but remember that your vocation, and every other area of your life, should contribute to rather than detract from your relationship with God.

Conclusion

As you have been reading this chapter, have you thought of ways to sharpen the vocational area of your own life? Do you know what God's calling for you is? If not, have you gone over the steps for determining God's will in this area that are outlined in Chapter 9? Have you sought appropriate training for whatever God has called you to do? Have you taken steps to supplement that training with actual experience in your vocation? Have you found someone with expertise in your field to learn from as you are gaining that experience? Are you "producing" yet? Do you do all "to the honor and glory of God," or do you simply "get by" with the least amount of time and effort possible? Are you willing to be "stretched" in your vocation? These and other concepts presented in this chapter are designed to cause you to think.

Whatever aspect of your vocational area of life needs improving is probably well worth improving due to the time you likely spend in your vocation. Satisfaction there tends to significantly impact the other areas of your life.

FOR YOUR FURTHER STUDY

Bolles, Richard. *What Color Is Your Parachute?* Walnut Creek, California: Tenspeed Press, revised annually.

Bradley, John D. *Christian Career Planning.* Portland, Oregon: Multnomah Press, 1977.

Campbell, David. *If You Don't Know Where You're Going You'll Probably End Up Somewhere Else.* Niles, Illinois: Argus Communications, 1974.

Dillow, Linda. *Creative Counterpart.* New York: Thomas Nelson Publishers, 1977.

The Directory of Christian Work Opportunity. Intercristo, Box 9323, Seattle, Washington 98109.

Schaeffer, Edith. *Hidden Art.* Wheaton: Tyndale House Publishers, 1975.

White, Jerry and Mary. *Your Job: Survival or Satisfaction?* Grand Rapids, Michigan: Zondervan Publishing House, 1977.

Zehring, John W. *Get Your Career in Gear.* Wheaton: Victor Books, 1976.

16

The Financial Area of Life

The Scriptures have a great deal to say about finances. There are more than 700 references to money in the Bible. Nearly two-thirds of the parables of Christ mention money or wealth in some way. Therefore, as Christians, we should be able to gain a great deal of financial wisdom from the Scriptures.

Perhaps the worst aspect of wealth is that it can harden our hearts toward God, as is outlined in Deuteronomy 8:10-14:

> When you have eaten and are satisfied, you shall bless the Lord your God for the good land which He has given you. Beware lest you forget the Lord your God by not keeping His commandments and His ordinances and His statutes which I am commanding you today; lest, when you have eaten and are satisfied, and have built good houses and lived in them, and when your herds and your flocks multiply, and your silver and gold multiply, and all that you have multiplies, then your heart becomes proud, and you forget

the Lord your God who brought you out from
the land of Egypt, out of the house of slavery.

Since money enables us to enjoy all kinds of worldly
goods, it can help us become attached to the world. In I John
2:15-17, we are warned against such a situation:

Do not love the world, nor the things in the world.
If any one loves the world, the love of the Father
is not in him. For all that is in the world, the lust of
the flesh and the lust of the eyes and the boastful
pride of life, is not from the Father, but is from the
world. And the world is passing away, and also its
lusts; but the one who does the will of God abides
forever.

What are we to do then? Avoid the use of money altogether? No, but we should carefully consider what God
would have us do with our money and then obey Him.

What follows is only a summary of the many scriptural
principles related to finances. I am hoping it will stimulate
your thinking and cause further study. As with the preceding
several chapters, be sure to have your notepaper out as you
read.

There are several excellent books, workbooks and seminars
available to the Christian on this subject. The material that
follows was substantially derived, with permission, from
Your Finances in Changing Times and *Christian Financial
Concepts* by Larry Burkett.[1] I was in close touch with him as
he was developing these and other materials and feel they are
very helpful in gaining the biblical view on this subject. The
first thing we need to see is God's perspective on the source
and ownership of financial resources.

Trust in God Not Man

We should trust God for all of our needs. In Matthew
6:33 we find: "But seek first His kingdom, and His righteous-

---

[1] Publishing information is at the end of this chapter.

ness; and all these things shall be added to you."

God is the ultimate source of everything that we will ever need in life. Our part is simply to trust and obey Him. The basis of our trust is God's promise to help us and provide for us, a promise which occurs frequently in the Scriptures. Psalms 50:15 is but one example: "And call upon Me in the day of trouble; I shall rescue you, and you will honor Me."

God may then lead you to take a very normal, practical course of action to meet your needs. The important thing is that you consult Him first and put your **trust** in Him.

What do we often do instead? Suppose we run short of money a few days before the end of the month. Most people use their charge cards or the automatic loan feature of their checking accounts without much hesitation or thought. How much better it would be if we would pause and pray for God's plan, acknowledging His promise to provide. He may encourage you to live with what He has already provided. He may send a special gift to you in some way to see you through. He may lead you to a way to supplement your income. The important thing is that you turned to God and put your trust in Him for your need.

Stewardship vs. Ownership

Second, we need to realize that we are not the "true owners" of what God has given us to use while on earth; we are merely the stewards of these things. Job spoke for all of us when he said: "Naked I came from my mother's womb, and naked I shall return there" (Job 1:21).

No matter how you look at it, there is nothing materially that any of us can bring into this world and nothing we can take out of it. So, while we are here, we simply manage certain things that God graciously entrusts to our stewardship. We are simply to take good care of what He has given us and make the maximum use of it for His glory.

The value of this perspective is quite clear. If we "own" something and then lose it, that is a source of great grief. If, however, we see ourselves as only stewards and are doing our best to take good care of God's possessions, a "loss" merely represents God's election to take something from our own stewardship and place it into someone else's. This is a matter of less concern for us if it was clear to us all along that it was God's and not ours. We then have fewer rights that can be affected. We can feel more freedom from the attachment to material things that plagues so many Christians. We are also more free to give material things away to those in greater need, which is something God may ask us to do.

Now, I would like to turn your attention from the basic perspective to the specific priority allocations of the income God gives you. The Scriptures seem to indicate four areas of disbursement that are to take priority over other potential disbursements. They are God's work, your family, your government and your debts.

The Priority of God's Work

If our objective as Christians is to glorify God, then obviously, financially contributing to His work here on earth is a priority for us.

This principle was illustrated long ago when Abram offered Melchizedek one-tenth of the spoils from the battle he had won (Genesis 14).

Specifically, the concept of the tithe is found throughout the Scriptures. Consider, for example, Leviticus 27:30: "Thus all the tithe of the land, of the seed of the land or of the fruit of the tree, is the Lord's; it is holy to the Lord."

In Proverbs 3:9,10 we are appraised that giving to God is not without personal blessing: "Honor the Lord from your wealth, and from the first of all your produce; so your barns will be filled with plenty, and your vats will overflow with new wine."

It seems that giving to God the first tenth of our income is an acknowledgement of His ultimate ownership of that income and of His benevolence in giving the income. In no way do the Scriptures limit us to 10%, but as you seek to allocate your income, it is a good practice to allocate the first 10% to God's work.

The Priority of Your Family

Paul tells us, "But if any one does not provide for his own, and especially for those of his household, he has denied the faith, and is worse than an unbeliever" (I Timothy 5:8).

God has promised to meet our needs, and if we are the provider for a household, He intends to provide for the needs of that household through us. I think it would be good to define the word "need" at this point. It means the basic provisions for living, such as adequate food, shelter, clothing, transportation, etc. Adequate food for good nutrition is a need; steak every night is not. Some sort of table on which to eat is a need; a television is not. God may well allow us to have many of our desires, and we will discuss that later. For now, though, I simply want to communicate that God **promised** to meet our **needs**. "And my God shall supply all your needs according to His riches in glory in Christ Jesus" (Philippians 4:19).

The Priority of Your Government

Romans 13:1-8 clearly cites the payment of all people their due as a priority for the allocation of our funds, and that includes the government that God has placed over us. Verses 6 and 7 state, "For because of this you also pay taxes, for rulers are servants of God, devoting themselves to this very thing. Render to all what is due them: tax to whom tax is due; custom to whom custom .... " Titus 3:1 reiterates the concept that Christians should be subject to the rulers and authorities over them.

The Priority of Your Debts

Very clear priority is given in Scripture to repaying our debts if we have the resources to do so. Consider Proverbs 3:27,28, "Do not withhold good from those to whom it is

due, when it is in your power to do it. Do not say to your
neighbor, 'Go and come back, and tomorrow I will give it,'
when you have it with you." And Psalms 37:21: "The wicked
borrows and does not pay back, but the righteous is gracious
and gives."

As a matter of fact, when we consider some of the negative
aspects of debt, it is a wonder that we venture into it very
often. Proverbs 22:7 points out the fact that the borrower
becomes the virtual slave of the lender. That usually mani-
fests itself in anxiety. If you've ever been over your head in
debt, you probably experienced that anxiety when you
looked at all your bills.

Perhaps more subtle, but equally as serious, is the principle
discussed in II Timothy 2:4. Paul explains here that it is very
difficult for a soldier in active service to do his duty properly
when he is entangled in the affairs of everyday life. Spiritually speaking, we are soldiers in God's army. We should avoid
entanglements with the things of this world that significantly
hamper our flexibility to do what He says.

This is not to say that borrowing money is absolutely
wrong under all circumstances. For example, when a person
buys a house, the law in his state may stipulate or he may be
able to arrange a contract whereby the lender will at any
time accept the house as full repayment of the obligation to
him. Then if the person cannot make the payments, and if,
for some very unlikely reason, he cannot sell the house over
a period of time, he has kept that problem from voiding his
ability to fund his other priorities.

In summary, God has promised to provide for our **needs**.
If we go into debt to buy or do something that is not a need,
we are presuming on God's willingness to provide over and
above our future needs in order to repay the debt. If He
chooses to give future income only according to our needs,
we then have to forgo meeting some of our needs in order
to repay the debt.

Repaying debts we have previously incurred is a priority
allocation of our funds before we allocate toward the possible other uses of our funds mentioned in the following

paragraphs.

Possibilities for Allocating Surplus

After we have taken care of all our priority areas with the funds that God has given us, we may well find ourselves with surplus funds. I think that in America today this should be the case for almost everyone. The reason many Americans think they are constantly short of funds is either that they define "need" very liberally or that they are so far in debt that repaying that debt is preempting current needs.

At any rate, when we do find ourselves in a position of surplus, we must decide how to allocate our extra funds. Let's look now at four possibilities recommended in the Scriptures: giving more to God's work, giving to the needs of others, investing for future needs and spending on your desires.

The Possibility of Giving More to God's Work

It is good to be in a position from which you can respond to a need in the area of God's work as you see it. This is especially gratifying when it is above and beyond what you initially allocated to His work in terms of your priority category above.

For example, I Corinthians 9:6-14 speaks of the importance of giving materially to those who minister to us spiritually. We see this in Luke 8:2,3, where some of the women healed of demon possession and other sicknesses are said to be contributing to the support of Jesus and His disciples.

The Possibility of Giving to the Needs of Others

II Corinthians 8:12-15 reveals God's formula for meeting the needs of His people:

> For if the readiness is present, it is acceptable
> according to what a man has, not according to
> what he does not have. For this is not for the

ease of others and for your affliction, but by
way of equality—at this present time your abundance being a supply for their want, that their
abundance also may become a supply for your
want, that there may be equality; as it is written,
He who gathered much did not have too much,
and he who gathered little had no lack.

From this Scripture we can deduce that at any given time
some of us will have a surplus. Part of God's plan to compensate for the initial deficit of those with a lack is for those
with a surplus to share from their abundance.

In the early church this was apparently common practice,
for in Acts 4:34 we are told there was not a single needy
person among the early Christians. Those who owned land or
houses sold them and brought the proceeds to the apostles
to distribute to their brothers and sisters in need.

If we do not share from our supply of the world's goods
as we ought, I John 3:17 tells us that the love of God does
not abide in us. And Proverbs 28:27 discloses the results of
both open-handedness and selfishness toward the needs of
others: "He who gives to the poor will never want, but he
who shuts his eyes will have many curses."

The Possibility of Investing for Future Needs

Consider Proverbs 21:20: "There is precious treasure and
oil in the dwelling of the wise, but a foolish man swallows it
up." And in Psalms 112:3 we find, "Wealth and riches are in
his house, and his righteousness endures forever."

Apparently, it is within the realm of God's plan that His
people set aside a reasonable amount from their income to
provide for future need. Such investment could be used for
a college education, for the children, or for a rainy day, such
as illness or unemployment. The only word of caution I
would have in this regard is that we could easily carry this
point too far in light of other ways we could allocate our
surplus funds.

The Possibility of Spending on Your Desires

There are portions of Scripture which suggest that God intends for us to enjoy good things in life. Consider, for example, the following verses:

> Furthermore, as for every man to whom God has given riches and wealth, He has also empowered him to eat from them and to receive his reward and rejoice in his labor; this is the gift of God. For He will not often consider the years of his life, because God keeps him occupied with the gladness of his heart (Ecclesiastes 5:19,20).

> I know how to get along with humble means, and I also know how to live in prosperity; in any and every circumstance I have learned the secret of being filled and going hungry, both of having abundance and suffering need (Philippians 4:12).

> Who satisfied your years with good things, so that your youth is renewed like the eagle (Psalms 103:5).

All of these passages suggest that God is sometimes willing to bless us with goods from the world even beyond our needs. Needless to say, however, this does not mean that we are to stop trusting God in times of abundance or that we should ever forget that He alone is the source of our good fortune.

Let me add, too, at this point that I suspect that we in America today satisfy our desires far beyond God's intentions, and that other areas in which we could be using our money suffer as a result.

How to Choose

The procedure for allocating our surplus funds is to consider all four of the potential areas of allocation at once. That is to say, we should carefully consider ways to use extra money to advance God's work, to meet the needs of others, to invest for future needs, and to satisfy current desires. Then we should prayerfully weigh the possibilities one against the other and decide how God would have us proceed.

The advantage of systematically considering all four areas of possible allocation at once is that God can more readily direct us as to His financial plan for our lives when we are open to **all** the possibilities. Otherwise the constant presence of our desires will tend to cause us to overspend on ourselves, particularly versus giving away as much money as God wants us to give.

How to Budget

Now that we have discussed **where** you should be spending your money, let's look at **how** you can be sure that it gets there.

Perhaps the most useful tool for bringing your finances under control is a budget. One of the very first things that my wife and I did in our married life was to come up with a budget for ourselves as a couple. We have revised that budget from time to time, but we still find it is the best way to prayerfully and thoughtfully determine what God would have us do with our money.

There are many types of budget worksheets available commercially, but if you need a place to start, there is a suggested budget form at the end of this chapter. You'll notice that this particular budget first allows for the allocation of funds for priority disbursements and then for the allocation of surplus.

Interestingly enough, when I taught this subject of financial management to my Sunday school class of college and career-age singles, we found that the single person earning a minimum wage in the state of California probably has more than $100 of monthly surplus over priorities.

This simply goes to show that, if we budget our needs very carefully, we will more than likely find ourselves in the very satisfying position of having to decide what to do with the surplus God has given us.

Some Money-saving Hints

There are many good books on the market that describe specific ways to stay within your budget and to save money. However, I would like to take time now to point out to you a few of the best ways.

First of all, it is important that you agree with your spouse and commit to yourself that you will purchase only in accordance with the guidelines you have established in your budget. For example, if you have planned to spend $30 a month on clothing, then that is all you should actually spend. You should keep track of what you are spending for clothing, and when your monthly clothes allotment runs out, you should wait until the next month to buy more or cut back specifically in another area of need. Don't "buy now and pay later."

Distinguish Between Need and Desire

Second, it is important that you constantly distinguish between need and desire. As you evaluate between different pieces of clothing or between different foods, or whatever, prayerfully consider what you really need versus what might be nice. Always consider what would bring maximum glory to God, and when you are considering a purchase, always weigh it against the other possible ways of using your money.

Third, the point of actual purchase is probably where we do or we don't bring our finances under control. I've made a tentative rule for myself not to buy any item that is relatively costly unless I have already determined that I need it, and then not before I have done some comparative shopping. This practice causes me to avoid "impulse buying." Impulse buying can destroy the budget. Pray and ask God to deliver you from being at the mercy of tempting advertisements and displays. You and God, not the salesperson, determine your need.

Fourth, in my home my wife and I are each responsible for different areas of the budget and we divide up our funds accordingly each month. For example, my wife purchases all of our food, all the gifts we give to others and a number of other items that she can easily pick up when she's out shopping. I am responsible for housing payments, auto expenses, insurance, etc.

Fifth, if you find that your income decreases for some reason, permanently or temporarily, make the necessary adjustment by lowering your level of expense, not by going into debt. In Philippians 4:12,13, Paul speaks of being able to adjust to either humble means or to prosperity with equal flexibility. Paul did not adjust to poverty through debt, but through Christ who strengthened him.

Take Time—Get a Good Buy

Sixth, don't rush yourself in the area of expense, and if you don't have peace, don't buy. Rather, "Rest in the Lord and wait patiently for Him" (Psalms 37:7) to lead you. As you shop, look for places where you can purchase quality items at lower prices. In time, you will learn which clothing, food and other stores in your community offer the best value for your money. My wife, for example, has found a place that carries very nice gift items which are relatively inexpensive. When she comes across an item that is a particularly good buy for a shower or wedding gift, she generally buys several of them at once. This procedure saves time as well as money.

Seventh, take advantage of sales. Planning allows you to know your needs in advance so that you can purchase goods when they are available at the lowest prices.

Eighth, when considering a major purchase, it is a good idea to consult *Consumer Reports* or some other impartial source to be sure of quality as well as savings.

Repair Versus Buying New

Ninth, as a further strategy for saving money, I recommend that you consider repairing damaged items as opposed to throwing them away and buying new. Most of the items we use in our daily lives, such as our cars and our appliances, can be readily repaired. Many people trade in their cars long before they become expensive to repair and inconvenient to operate.

Tenth, as one last thought on the subject of saving money, I'd like to address the subject of charge cards. If you are a person of great discipline who can use charge cards as a convenience rather than as a financial crutch, then by all means use them. If, however, you are like so many others who use charge cards to buy things that they really cannot afford at the moment, but which they figure they'll somehow pay for later, then I recommend you don't use them. They make it far too easy for you to violate the plans you have prayerfully made for your money.

Conclusion

Though we are bombarded daily with suggestions as to how we should spend our money, we as Christians have a responsibility to make an aggressive, concentrated effort to conform to God's plan for our finances instead of the world's plan. The financial area of our lives provides an excellent opportunity to trust and to obey God, and as we do this, we reap the benefits both spiritually and materially.

If you have learned some things you particularly want to implement soon, be sure to write them on your notepaper before proceeding.

SAMPLE BUDGET WORKSHEET
(Referred to in the chapter)

I. **PRIORITY DISBURSEMENTS**

God's Work
(specify ministry)

_____   _____
_____   _____
_____   _____

Family Needs

House payments (including tax,
insurance) or rent   _____

Utilities   _____

Food   _____

Clothing   _____

Transportation (including pay-
ments, gas, repairs, insurance, etc.)   _____

Toiletries   _____

Household purchases   _____

Other insurance   _____

Phone   _____

Entertainment   _____

Gifts   _____

Education   _____

Cleaning/laundry   _____

General repairs   _____

Vacation   _____

Miscellaneous   _____

Government (Income tax,
social security)   _____

Debt reduction   _____

TOTAL PRIORITY DISBURSEMENTS   _____

II.   SURPLUS CALCULATION
     Gross Income   _____
     (minus) Total priority disbursements   _____
     (equals) Surplus   _____

III. ALLOCATION OF SURPLUS
     God's Work

     _____   _____

     _____   _____

     Needs of Others

     _____   _____

     _____   _____

     Investments

     _____   _____

     _____   _____

     Desires

     _____   _____

     _____   _____

            TOTAL SURPLUS   _____

FOR YOUR FURTHER STUDY

Bowman, George E. *How to Succeed with Your Money.* Chicago: Moody Press, 1960, revised 1974.

Burkett, Larry. *Christian Financial Concepts.* San Bernardino, California: Campus Crusade for Christ, 1975.

Burkett, Larry. *Your Finances in Changing Times.* San Bernardino, California: Campus Crusade for Christ, 1975.

Dowd, Merle. *How to Live Better and Spend 20% Less.* West Nyack, New York: Parker Publishing Co., Inc., 1967.

Fooshee, George. *You Can Be Financially Free.* Old Tappan, New Jersey: Fleming H. Revell Co., 1976.

Galloway, Dale E. *There Is a Solution to Your Money Problems.* Glendale, California: Regal Books Division, G/L Publications, 1977.

Kilgore, James, with Highlander, Don. *Getting More Family Out of Your Dollar.* Irvine, California: Harvest House Publications, 1976.

McLean, Gordon. *Let God Manage Your Money.* Grand Rapids, Michigan: Zondervan Publishing House, 1972.

Poriss, Martin. *How to Live Cheap but Good.* New York: Dell Publishing Co., 1971.

Seminars: Winning the Money Battle. Christian Financial Ministries, 3518 Carlsbad Blvd., Carlsbad, California 92008, David Hornberger, President.

Christian Financial Concepts, 4730 Darlene Way, Tucker, Georgia 30084, Larry Burkett, President.

17

The Family Area of Life

After He had created the heavens and the earth and everything in them, God looked at His creation and proclaimed that it was good. Then He looked at Adam's situation and proclaimed, "It is not good for the man to be alone" (Genesis 2:18). In the process of solving Adam's problem, God created the first, closest and most basic of all social institutions—marriage. "For this cause a man shall leave his father and mother, and shall cleave to his wife, and they shall become one flesh" (Genesis 2:24).

Marriage and Family as Illustrations

The marriage relationship is important in other ways than its firstness and closeness, however. For one thing, it serves as an illustration in God's revelation to man. Consider, for example, Ephesians 5:23: "For the husband is the head of the wife, as Christ also is the head of the church . . . ." And Ephesians 5:25: "Husbands, love your wives, just as Christ also loved the church . . . . " By observing a marriage that is functioning according to God's standards, we get a glimpse of the proper relationship between God and man.

The marriage relationship is most often blessed with children; these are to be considered a "gift of the Lord" and a "reward" (Psalms 127:3). The child-parent relationship is also an illustration used in the revelation of spiritual truth. For example, just as the earthly father seeks to raise his children to responsible adulthood, nurturing them along and training them up in the way they should go, so does God seek to bring all new Christians to full maturity in Christ in many of the same ways.

From the child's point of view, the earthly father provides the first indication of what the heavenly Father is like. The child later learns that, just as he is to "honor (his) father and (his) mother," so is he to honor God by obeying His instructions.

From the parents' standpoint, the relationship with a child can be very revealing in terms of how man should behave in his relationship with God. Much of what a parent hopes for and expects from his children is what God hopes for and expects from all of us.

Needless to say, unless a marriage, or any family relationship, is functioning in accordance with God's standards, it does not provide an accurate witness of the proper relationship between God and man. Therefore it is important that these relationships function as God intended.

In this chapter, we will examine the normal sequence of a person from singlehood to marriage to parenthood. As we consider various decisions and responsibilities, see if there are areas in which you can improve. In some cases I will give some specific thoughts to consider, and in others I will simply ask you some questions to help stimulate your thinking. As before, you might find it valuable to make a note of anything that seems to speak particularly to your own situation.

Should You Marry?

The first question a single person should resolve in regard

to marriage is if God would have him marry at all. Although marriage is a very special and beneficial relationship, and is God's will for most of us, I Corinthians 7 does point out the unequaled flexibility and availability for service of those who are unmarried.

Of course, there is no magic age at which the question of whether or not to marry needs be resolved once and for all. I personally spent several years as a single adult before concluding that God truly did intend for me to marry. But it is important that the young single person at least consider the possibility that God, in His wisdom, might want him to remain single.

Whom Should You Marry?

If God does, in fact, lead the single person to marry, as is usually the case, then the question shifts from "whether" to "which one." After the decision of knowing Christ in a personal way, the choice of a life's mate is the most important decision we ever make, for if we are to live by God's standards, it is an irreversible one. We cannot experiment with marriage as we can with a career, for example. Therefore, the decision of whom to marry warrants a great deal of prayer, clear thinking and, finally, unqualified obedience to God.

And yet, what often happens? Young man meets young woman. There is a strong attraction. Before too long they are engaged. Not that emotions and love, or any of the vibrations associated with the time of courtship and marriage, are wrong—far from it. It is simply important that a person takes time to prayerfully think through the implications of an entire life with a particular person before making a final decision to marry him or her.

A person might find, for example, that God has given both parties a real sense of calling, but the respective callings are not headed in the same direction. Such a situation would be a pretty good sign that the two people were not meant for each other.

Or perhaps, as the couple thinks about it, they do not find each other stimulating mentally, or are frequently in disagreement on basic subjects. These situations, too, would be warning signals as to their incompatibility.

One very basic qualification for a spouse is that he, or she, be able to be a person's closest friend, for in God's economy, that's part of what husbands and wives should be—closest friends. If you are single, be sure you marry someone with whom you can be closest friends.

Develop the Relationship

Once you have decided to marry, have chosen your mate and have indeed been joined as one, you need to be committed to the full development of your relationship. Whatever thought and effort you give toward befriending others should be exceeded by the thought and effort you give to maintaining a close relationship with your spouse. Your marriage relationship is your highest priority, as far as human relationships go.

As you seek to build your marriage, you will find that certain things contribute to the closeness of your relationship, and other things detract from it. Careful attention should be given to maximizing these things that do contribute, and to eliminating as many as possible of those things that detract.

In Campus Crusade for Christ, husbands and wives are encouraged to set aside time each year for "planning weekends"—mini-vacation-planning sessions spent away from the children and apart from the distraction of the day to day. Partners are encouraged to communicate, with the aid of specially prepared materials, on a variety of topics, many of which they might not otherwise have an opportunity to talk about in the course of their busy lives. They are encouraged to study the Scriptures together and come to agreement on issues that are key to them. For as Amos 3:3 (King James Bible) points out, "Can two walk together except they be agreed?"

During planning sessions such as this, and indeed throughout their marriages, couples are encouraged to find out specifically what does and what does not please the other person. This knowledge serves to equip each party to meet the other's needs better.

Every year since we have been married, my wife and I have taken a planning weekend. Each time we have discussed what we felt God was leading us to emphasize in our lives, both as a couple and individually, over the next six to twelve months. Then, we set objectives for ourselves accordingly.

We have found that two heads are truly better than one in this process. It is very helpful to share with each other thoughts and insights that we probably would not have come up with on our own. Also, as we decide together on various courses of action, we are prepared to pray for and encourage each other specifically during the year, to keep up with the other's progress, to offer helpful hints as we think of them and to make allowances for one another as we each seek to improve in various areas of our lives.

A significant part of the closeness of marriage has to do with physical intimacy. As the two partners become one flesh, God provides a special sense of union with each other that is very important to the relationship. If either you or your spouse feels that your physical relationship is not adequate, then I would encourage you to seek help in this area. There is a great deal of Christian material available on the subject, and personal counseling is also available in most communities.

In summary, are you seeking to develop your relationship with your spouse? What specific actions could you take to become more of a close friend to him or her? What one thing could you easily do right away?

Love One Another

"Beloved, let us love one another," starts one of the major biblical passages on love in I John 4:7-21. One of the key ingredients in any successful relationship, and particularly in a marriage, is love. God's quality of love is the cement that binds people together; it enables them to overcome any barrier and ride out any storm in a relationship.

I once had the occasion to help out a friend of mine who was having trouble with her roommate. Although I have to admit there were many things the roommate should have been doing differently, I encouraged my friend to take the initiative. I suggested that she take out a piece of paper and block off three columns. In the first column, she wrote down the various qualities of love—patience, kindness, lack of jealousy, etc.—that are listed in I Corinthians 13:4-8. In the second column, she wrote down the ways in which she was **not** conforming to the qualities in relation to her roommate. Then, in the third column, I helped her think of creative ways she **could** conform to the qualities.

As we worked down the page, we eventually came up with a list of many specific things my friend could do every day to demonstrate love for her roommate in a tangible way. A number of weeks later, when I asked her how things were going, she said, "Better than ever before!"

Are you taking the initiative to tangibly show your love for your spouse along the lines of the biblical specifications of love?

Marriage: Communication or Chaos

Another key ingredient in any good relationship, and particularly in a marriage, is communication. No one I know of has better advice on this subject than Dallas Theological Seminary Professor Dr. Howard G. Hendricks. I once heard an excellent talk he gave on the subject: "Marriage: Communication or Chaos."[1] I am grateful for his permission to share a few of his thoughts from the talk with you here:

Accent understanding rather than talking. In conversations with your spouse, concentrate on listening.

---

[1] Publishing information is at the end of the chapter.

Underscore in your mind what is important to your spouse or what might be troubling him or her. Maintain an attitude of, "May I seek more to understand than to be understood."

Develop common interests. The more activities you participate in jointly, the greater will be your communication. Look for recreational activities that you would enjoy doing together and pursue them. Know something about each other's work. Remember that only about one-half of your married life will be spent with children in the home, and you will have many years together alone. Therefore, seek true companionship and learn to enjoy each other as an investment in your future.

Make yourself an interesting and attractive person. Read widely to develop your knowledge and interest in a variety of subjects. Keep abreast of what is going on so that you will be stimulating to talk to.

Set aside specific times for communication. Share needs, express opinions, make requests, etc. Also study the Word of God and pray together as a couple and as a family. Set goals together and then come up with a cooperative plan to reach those goals. Evaluate your relationship with each member of the family and determine ways you can make any necessary improvements.

In summary, how is your communication with your spouse? When is the last time you had a special time to talk about where you are going as a couple and how you can help each other better? When are you going to plan to have the next such communication session?

Should You Have Children?

Now let's turn from the topic of marriage to the topic of children.

One of the key issues a married couple should resolve is whether or not God wants them to have children. Normally,

God does include children as part of the family unit, but they are not necessarily a part of His plan for every couple. To raise children properly takes a great deal of time. Such an investment of time deserves to be weighed carefully in light of whatever else God has called a couple to do. On the other hand, children are a great source of joy and fulfillment and they are a very tangible way God can show His love for us.

A Great Responsibility and a Lot of Fun

If God does lead you as a couple to have children, there is a very definite responsibility that goes with the privilege, and that is to raise those children according to God's standards. Compared to the adult relationships you have, your relationships with your children make more demands on you. A child has many needs and no ability to help you at first. Therefore your love must be even more prepared to give than it is in your other relationships.

In his book on the art and joy of successful family living, *Heaven Help the Home,*[2] Dr. Hendricks cites 12 ways in which you can live up to your responsibility as a parent and "remodel your house into a home," if it is not one already. His suggestions are as follows:

1. Review the status of each member of the household to see that everyone feels he is a VIP in the family. He can believe in himself because this "in" group where he lives likes him, accepts him and trusts him for himself.
2. Check the basic structure. Dad is to be the head, Mother transparently supporting him, and the children all sharing responsibilities.
3. Scrutinize family values. A dominant, unifying focal theme is needed. Anything other than Jesus Christ is too weak for permanent cohesion. A personal commitment to Christ, backed up with positive reasons, should be the parental example. At some point, every

---

[2] Hendricks, Howard. *Heaven Help the Home.* Wheaton: Victor Books, 1974, pp. 141-142.

member should be privately confronted with the claims of Christ on his life.

4. Develop family pride through accomplishment with skill and talent. Plant the seeds with music lessons, hobbies, good books. Use every ability God gave you.

5. Build up the fun-side of the family with laughter at mistakes and imaginative recreational pastimes. A positive, constructive home is magnetic.

6. Ease up on forced togetherness. Give each one encouragement to be away sometimes. At home, provide privacy to foster personal relationship with God.

7. Overhaul the emotional air conditioning system. Avoid charging the atmosphere with tension. Keep the home ventilated with positive comments and relaxed attitudes.

8. Sweep out old grudges like worthless debris. Forgive and forget the past, "even as Christ has forgiven you."

9. Renew the outlets, so that the family is wired for positive communication. A free exchange of ideas, without condemnation, is essential. Remember that communication is largely by life, not by lecture.

10. Keep the door open to family friends, allowing the fragrance of a virile Christian home to benefit others.

11. Expect periodic spills of immaturity and imperfection. Clean them up with firm, calm, reasonable discipline. Plan a "better way" for next time. Let out enough developmental rope to allow each individual not to hang himself, but to tie a few of his own knots.

12. Allow the Holy Spirit to make you authentically like Christ. No artificial front can stand the daily erosion of home life. What you are is far more important than what you say.

How are you doing with your children? Are you committed to the time and effort needed to raise them properly? Are they confident of your love for them and belief in them? Do you study the Bible and pray together with your children? Does your family really enjoy being together? What one thing could you do to improve your relationship with your children?

Help Your Children to Plan

As your children become old enough, teach them to set objectives for themselves prayerfully and then help them come up with ways to meet those objectives. These objectives can relate to improvement areas in the children's lives or to some other accomplishment that is especially meaningful to them. This puts them in the position of seeking to improve versus resisting rules and regulations that you might otherwise establish to achieve the same improvement. This gives children specific things to ask God for themselves.

Even if your children are too young for this, it is important that you and your spouse carefully think through what areas of emphasis you are going to have with each child each year. Think of ways to cultivate positive character traits. Praise God for the strengths He has already built into their temperaments and characters, and pray for your children in their areas of weakness.

The Family as a Team

It would be impossible to conclude any discussion about the family without pointing out that it is not a group of random individuals sharing a common roof, but is rather a closely knit team, bound together by a common purpose and a cooperative plan. Of course, the common purpose should be to glorify Christ, and the cooperative plan should consist of ways in which the family, both individually and as a unit, can best achieve that purpose.

Think through the various areas of your life—the spiritual, mental, physical, social, vocational and financial—and see if there are ways in which you could involve your whole family in these areas.

In the spiritual domain, for example, how could you include your spouse and your children in your devotional life? What about church activities? Can you become involved in a way that would include the whole family?

In the physical area of life, is it possible to exercise in a way that can involve at least some of the rest of the family? I know men who run in the morning with their sons. I know couples who play tennis together. I once heard a speaker mention that he gave up one of his favorite sports because it took so much of his time away from his family. Instead, he switched to an activity that they could all do together and have fellowship in the process.

As you consider the social area of your life, are you bringing to your home and involving your children with people who are good examples of Christians? Are there friends and acquaintances for whom you could pray together as a family?

Conclusion

Our families are both a great blessing and a great responsibility. We should carefully consider our decisions with regard to marriage and children. We should make provision for the time and energy needed to develop our family relationships. We should enjoy our families.

Before leaving this chapter, be sure to write down any concepts that have been particularly meaningful and applicable to you.

FOR YOUR FURTHER STUDY

Bock, Lois and Working, Miji. *Happiness Is a Family Time Together*. Old Tappan, New Jersey: Fleming H. Revell Co., 1975.

Brandt, Henry and Landrum, Phil. *I Want My Marriage to Be Better*. Grand Rapids: Zondervan Publishing House, 1976.

Cooper, Darien B. *You Can Be the Wife of a Happy Husband.* Wheaton: Victor Books, 1974.

Dobson, James. *Dare to Discipline.* Wheaton: Tyndale House Publishers, 1970.

Dodson, Fitzhugh. *How to Parent.* New York: New American Library, 1973.

Hendricks, Howard G. *Heaven Help the Home.* Wheaton: Victor Books, 1974.

Hendricks, Howard G. "Marriage: Communication or Chaos." Cassette tapes: Here's Life Publishers, Campus Crusade for Christ, San Bernardino, California 92414.

MacDonald, Gordon. *Effective Father.* Wheaton: Tyndale House Publishers, 1977.

Schaeffer, Edith. *What Is a Family?* Old Tappan, New Jersey: Fleming H. Revell Co., 1975.

Wheat, Ed and Gaye. *Intended for Pleasure.* Old Tappan, New Jersey: Fleming H. Revell Co., 1977.

Wright, H. Norman. *Communication: Key to Your Marriage.* Glendale, California: Regal Books Division, G/L Publications, 1974.

18

Conclusion

In Part II we have discussed more in-depth concepts of managing yourself. As they become particularly helpful to you at new levels and complexities of your activities, I trust you will take advantage of them. I have often had just that one new idea greatly increase my effectiveness at a given time. View this entire book as a reference to you so that, when you embark on some new venture, you can review the relevant chapters for time-saving and effectiveness-increasing ideas.

In this concluding chapter, I would like to remind you of and encourage you to apply some of the main points of personal management.

Keep walking closely with God, both to discern His wisdom for you and to have the power to do what He asks of you. Don't let unconfessed sin accumulate. Enjoy your fellowship with God and the comfort of His constant guidance. This walk is more key than anything else to managing yourself.

God does have a plan for your life. How very important it is for you to know as much of it as He chooses to reveal at this time. A life without aim is a life destined to failure and discouragement.

Stay sensitive to time. It is a very valuable resource that God has given to you. Once you have spent it on something that wasn't worth it, you cannot retrieve it. Know what is priority and then seek to do it.

Continue to pray for God's help in keeping you motivated to do the priorities. An enjoyable life is made up of enjoyable moments, hours and days.

Don't be afraid of discipline as God increases this quality in your life. It is not possible even to grow as a Christian without a willingness to do a new activity for the first time and finally form it into a habit.

Seek to achieve the point in your daily life at which you sense your life is under control, at which, with God's guidance, you are able to choose and stick to those activities that are truly productive toward God's objectives for you.

Don't so overextend yourself that, in effect, you reduce to low priority your walk with God, your health, your peace of mind or your family. God's calling for you is not inconsistent with scriptural priorities. I have found, though, that as I increasingly "manage myself" I am able to have a better walk with God, better health, more peace of mind, a better relationship with my wife and, at the same time, greater effectiveness in my vocation.

Don't stop praying and thinking about what you do and what is going on around you. The minute you do is the minute you start dying mentally. So much of what I have shared with you is a direct result of a lifestyle of asking questions, of myself and of others. Seek to be prayerful and creative in facing your problems.

In closing, my prayer for you is that God will never let you settle for anything less than His best for your life.

FOR YOUR FURTHER STUDY

Alexander, John W. *Managing Our Work*. Downers Grove, Illinois: Inter-Varsity Press, 1972.

Cook, William H. *Success, Motivation and the Scriptures*. Nashville: Broadman Press, 1974.

Dayton, Edward R. *Tools for Time Management*. Grand Rapids: Zondervan Publishing House, 1974.

Dayton, Edward R. and Engstrom, Ted W. *Strategy for Living*. Glendale, California: Regal Books, 1976.

Douglass, Stephen B. and Cook, Bruce E. *The Ministry of Management*. San Bernardino, California: Campus Crusade for Christ, 1972.

Eims, Leroy. *Be the Leader You Were Meant to Be*. Wheaton: Victor Books Division, SP Publications, Inc., 1976.

Engstrom, Ted W. and Mackenzie, R. Alec. *Managing Your Time*. Grand Rapids: Zondervan Publishing House, 1967.

Hummel, Charles E. *Tyranny of the Urgent*. Downers Grove: Inter-Varsity Press, 1967.

Lakein, Alan. *How to Get Control of Your Time and Your Life*. Peter H. Wyden, Inc., 1973.

Mackenzie, R. Alec. *The Time Trap*. New York: McGraw-Hill, 1972.

Sanders, J. Oswald. *Spiritual Leadership*. Chicago: Moody Press, 1967.